Progress™

Mathematics

1

S Sadlier School

W9-BKF-654

Cover: *Series Design:* Studio Montage; *Title design:* Quarasan, Inc. **Photo Credits:** Cover: Corbis/Scott Speakes: *top left.* Getty Images/Jill Buschlen: *bottom left;* Tim Hall: *bottom right;* Purestock: *top right.* Used under license from Shutterstock.com/RoboLab: *background.* Interior: Alamy/PhotosIndia.com LLC: 8 *top.* Corbis/Scott Speakes: vi *center.* Dreamstime.com/Viktor Gladkov: vi *top right.* Getty Images/Asia Images: 160 *top;* Dorling Kindersley: 161; Maskot: 206 *top;* Mint Images - Frans Lanting: 9; Tetra Images: 94 *top.* Punchstock/Photographer's Choice: 95. Used under license from Shutterstock.com/axz700: 207 *bottom;* Elenamiv: 207 *background;* elisekurenbina: vi *bottom left;* FocusDzign: vi *top left;* Jana Guothova: 8 *bottom,* 94 *bottom,* 160 *bottom,* 206 *bottom;* Ian 2010: vi *bottom right;* Frank L Junior: 207 *top;* pjhpix: 207 *center;* RoboLab: 1, vi *background.* **Text Credit:** Common Core State Standards Copyright © 2010. National Governors Association Center for Best Practices and Council of Chief State School Officers. All rights reserved. **Illustrator Credit:** Bob Holt

For additional online resources, go to sadlierconnect.com.

William H. Sadlier, Inc.
9 Pine Street
New York, NY 10005-4700

Printed in the United States of America.
ISBN: 978-1-4217-3151-3
1 2 3 4 5 6 7 8 9 WEBC 18 17 16 15 14

Contents

Unit 4   Focus on Geometry

Welcome

You have an exciting year ahead of you. You will be learning about mathematics and the tools you will need to solve problems.

Did you know that you solve problems and use math every day? When you play sports, go shopping, cook, build something, or travel in a car, bus or train, you are using math.

Progress Mathematics will help you improve your math skills. With it, you may even do better in school. That's why the book is called *Progress*.

Have a great year!

Progress Check

Look at how the math concepts and skills you have learned and will learn connect.

To practice your skills, go to sadlierconnect.com.

GRADE K		GRADE 1		GRADE 2
I Can...	Before Unit 1	**Can I ?**	After Unit 1	**I Will...**
Solve word problems by adding or subtracting within 10	☐	Solve word problems by adding and subtracting within 20	☐	Solve one- and two-step word problems by adding and subtracting within 100
	☐	Use objects, drawings, and equations to represent word problems	☐	Use drawings and equations to represent word problems
	☐	Solve word problems by adding three numbers	☐	Add up to four two-digit numbers
Take apart numbers up to 10 Find the number that makes 10	☐	Use properties to add and subtract	☐	Explain why addition and subtraction strategies work
	☐	Relate subtraction to finding an unknown addend	☐	Understand and use the relationship between addition and subtraction
Count by ones Count from a given number	☐	Relate counting to addition and subtraction	☐	
Fluently add and subtract within 5	☐	Fluently add and subtract within 10	☐	Fluently add and subtract within 20
	☐	Add and subtract within 20	☐	Fluently add and subtract within 100
Show addition and subtraction with equations	☐	Tell if equations involving addition and subtraction are true or false	☐	
	☐	Find the unknown number in an addition or subtraction equation	☐	Understand and use the relationship between addition and subtraction

HOME ◆ CONNECT...

In first grade, your child will need to be able to add and subtract quickly and accurately. Your child will need to know addition and subtraction facts. Understanding the relationship between addition and subtraction is very important. One of the strategies your child will use for adding and subtracting quickly is related facts. When adding, your child can use a related subtraction fact. When subtracting, your child can use a related addition fact. Related facts use the same numbers.

For example, to solve $10 - \square = 5$, first write a related addition fact. $5 + \square = 10$

Then, find the missing number in the related addition sentence.

$5 + 5 = 10$ so the missing number is 5.
$10 - 5 = 5$

Activity: Practice addition and subtraction facts with your child. This practice will help your child be able to add and subtract quickly and accurately. Create real-world word problems for your child to solve. For example, you might say, "I need five potatoes for dinner. I have two potatoes already. How many more potatoes do we need to buy?" These kinds of questions will encourage discussions about Math.

In this unit your child will:

- Solve problems using addition and subtraction.
- Add three numbers.
- Relate addition and subtraction.
- Relate counting to addition and subtraction.
- Fluently add and subtract within 10.
- Add and subtract within 20.
- Find missing numbers in equations.
- Determine if an equation is true or false.

Ways to Help Your Child

The first grade math classroom will have many manipulatives to help the children understand math concepts. These manipulatives may be physical objects, such as counters and cubes. Or they may be virtual versions that are available in online libraries or as apps. When you visit your child's classroom, explore the manipulatives available. You may want to purchase or recreate some of these manipulatives for use at home.

ONLINE
For more Home Connect activities, continue online at sadlierconnect.com

Focus on Operations and Algebraic Thinking

Essential Question:
How are addition and subtraction related?

Problem Solving: Addition

Essential Question:
How can you use addition to solve word problems?

Words to Know
add

Guided Instruction

In this lesson you will learn how to add to solve word problems.

Understand: Add to find how many in all

> Lucy has 4 apples.
> José has 3 apples.
> How many apples in all?

You add to find how many in all.

| Lucy's apples | José's apples | How many in all? |

$$4 \quad + \quad 3 \quad = \quad 7$$

▷ There are 7 apples in all.

John has 2 marbles.
Kate has 4 marbles.
How many marbles do they have in all?

You can draw a picture to help you solve the problem.

John's marbles 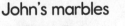 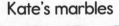   Kate's marbles

$$2 + 4 = 6$$

John and Kate have 6 marbles in all.

Guided Instruction

Understand: Sometimes you need to find how many in one of the groups

There are 6 butterflies in the garden.
Some more butterflies flew in.
Now there are 9 butterflies.
How many more butterflies flew into the garden?

6 butterflies   some more flew in   9 butterflies in all

6 plus how many more will make 9?

6 and 3 more make 9.

$$6 + 3 = 9$$

▷ _____ more butterflies flew into the garden.

Ken has 6 blocks.
His friend Joe gives him some more blocks.
Now Ken has 10 blocks.
How many blocks did Joe give Ken?
Draw a picture to help you solve the problem.

blocks Ken had   blocks Joe gave Ken

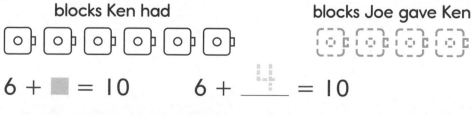

$$6 + \blacksquare = 10 \qquad 6 + \underline{} = 10$$

Joe gave Ken 4 blocks.

Guided Instruction

Connect: **What you know about adding to solve word problems**

There are 12 children on the swings.
Some are girls and 7 are boys.
How many girls are on the swings?

Step 1

How many children in all? __12__

How many boys? __7__

Use ■ for the number of girls.

■ + 7 = 12

Step 2

You can use connecting cubes to help you find the missing number.

How many plus 7 equals 12?

5 plus 7 equals 12.

5 + 7 = 12

▷ There are ____ girls on the swings.

Guided Practice

**1. Ryan has 8 balloons.
Some are red and some are blue.
How many of each color can Ryan have?**

Step 1

To solve this problem you need to find two numbers that make 8.

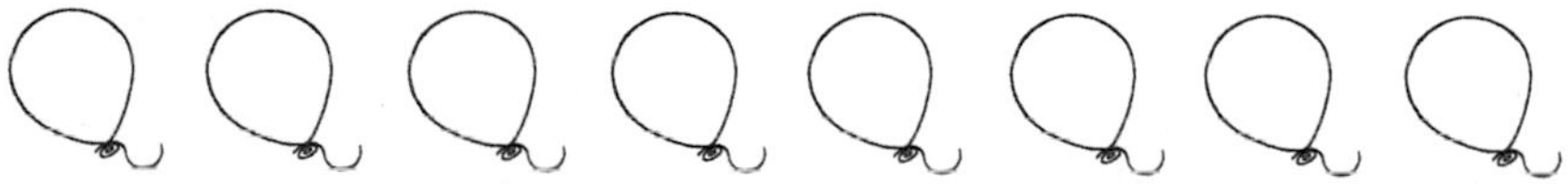

Decide on how many red balloons he has.
Color 4 balloons red.

Step 2

Color the rest of the balloons blue.

How many balloons are blue? 4

4 (red) + 4 (blue) = 8

➡ Ryan has ____ red balloons and ____ blue balloons.

Think•Pair•Share

MP4 **2.** Draw a picture to show another way to solve the balloon problem. Then use addition to solve it.

____ + ____ = ____ balloons

Independent Practice

Draw a picture to help you solve each problem.

1. Five boys are on the bus.
   Two more boys get on.
   How many boys are on the bus now?

   How many boys are on the bus at the start? ____

   How many more get on? ____
   How many boys are on the bus now?

   $5 + 2 = $ ____

   There are ____ boys on the bus now.

2. Three girls are at the park.
   Some more girls come to the park.
   Now there are 10 girls at the park.
   How many more girls came to the park?

   $3 + $ ____ $ = 10$

   ____ more girls came to the park.

Independent Practice

Draw a picture to help you solve each problem.

3. Six players are on the field.
   Three more players come onto the field.
   How many players are on the field now?

   6 + 3 = ____

   There are ____ players on the field now.

4. Some birds were in the tree.
   Five more birds flew over.
   Then there were 13 birds in the tree.
   How many birds were in the tree before?

   ____ + 5 = 13

   ____ birds were in the tree before.

5. There are 15 crayons on the table.
   Eight of them are red.
   The rest are yellow.
   How many crayons are yellow?

   8 + ____ = 15

   There are ____ yellow crayons.

Independent Practice

Draw a picture to help you solve each problem.

6. Nine toys were in the toy box.
   Max puts some more toys in the box.
   Now there are 18 toys in the box.
   How many toys did Max put in the box?

   ____ + ____ = ____

   Max put ____ toys in the box.

7. Some cars were parked in the garage.
   Seven more cars drove in.
   Now there are 11 cars parked there.
   How many cars were parked there before?

   ____ + ____ = ____

   ____ cars were parked there before.

8. Twelve fruits are in the basket.
   Some of the fruits are oranges.
   Eight of the fruits are apples.
   How many oranges are in the basket?

   ____ + ____ = ____

   There are ____ oranges in the basket.

Independent Practice

Draw a picture to help you solve each problem.

9. Some ducks are in the pond.
   Six more ducks fly to the pond.
   Now there are 11 ducks in the pond.
   How many ducks were in the pond before?

   _____ ducks were in the pond before.

10. There are 7 black sheep and 8 white sheep
    in the barn. How many sheep are there in all?

    There are _____ sheep in all.

MP1 11. Kim has five books.
    Some are old and some are new.
    How many can be old and how many
    can be new?

    $\dfrac{}{\text{old}} + \dfrac{}{\text{new}} = \underline{}$ books

    Talk about other possible answers.

Problem Solving: Subtraction

Essential Question:
How can you use subtraction to solve word problems?

Words to Know
subtract

Guided Instruction

In this lesson you will use subtraction to solve word problems.

Understand: Sometimes you need to find how many are left

Robin has 6 bananas.
She gives 4 of them to her friends.
How many bananas does she have now?

You can subtract to find how many are left.

6   –   4   = ▪

6 take away 4 is 2.

$6 - 4 = 2$

➡ Robin has 2 bananas now.

Sam has 7 stickers. He gives 3 stickers to Juan.
How many stickers does Sam have left?
Draw a picture to help you solve the problem.

◯ ◯ ◯ ◯ ⊗ ⊗ ⊗

$7 - 3 = 4$

Sam has 4 stickers left.

Guided Instruction

Understand: Sometimes you need to find how many things have been taken away

Ian sees 13 frogs.
Some of them hop away.
Now there are 8 frogs left.
How many frogs hop away?

How many frogs in all? 13

How many frogs are left? 8

You can subtract to find how many are taken away.

frogs in all	some hop away	frogs left
13	− ▦	= 8

Find the missing number.

You can use connecting cubes to help you.

13 take away how many leaves 8?

13 take away 5 is 8.

$$13 - 5 = 8$$

⇨ _____ frogs hop away.

Guided Instruction

Connect: Use subtraction to compare

There are 5 yellow flowers and 8 red flowers.
How many more red flowers are there
than yellow flowers?

Step 1

Start with what you know.

How many red flowers are there? _____

How many yellow flowers are there? _____

Step 2

Match each yellow flower with a red flower.

How many did you match? _____

Subtract to find how many more red flowers.

8 − 5 = 3

⇨ There are _____ more red flowers
than yellow flowers.

You can also say there are _____ fewer yellow
flowers than red flowers.

Guided Practice

1. **Bapi has 6 fewer baseball cards than Dan.
Dan has 11 baseball cards.
How many cards does Bapi have?**

Step 1

Start with the cards Dan has.
How many cards does Dan have? __11__
Draw Dan's cards.

Step 2

How many fewer cards does Bapi have? __6__
Cross off 6 cards.

Use subtraction to solve the problem.

$11 - 6 =$ _____

Bapi has _____ cards.

☼ Think•Pair•Share

MP1 2. Make up a problem you can solve using
subtraction. Draw a picture to show
your problem. Then solve the problem.

Independent Practice

Draw a picture to help you solve each problem.

1. Nine children are in class. Then 3 children leave. How many children are left in the class?

   How many children started in class? ____

   How many children leave? ____

   Subtract to find how many children are left.

   9 – 3 = ____

   There are ____ children left in the class.

2. Eleven apples were on the tree. Some fell off.
   Now there are 8 apples on the tree.
   How many apples fell off the tree?

   How many apples were on the tree to start? ____

   How many apples are on the tree now? ____

   Subtract to find how many apples fell off the tree.

   11 – ____ = 8

   ____ apples fell off the tree.

Independent Practice

Draw a picture to help you solve each problem.

3. There are 10 plates on the table.
Meg takes away 5 plates.
How many plates are left on the table?

$10 - 5 =$ _____

_____ plates are left on the table.

4. Tony has 15 crayons.
Sue has 8 crayons.
How many more crayons
does Tony have than Sue?

$15 - 8 =$ _____

Tony has _____ more crayons than Sue.

5. There are 9 more oranges than apples.
There are 16 oranges.
How many apples are there?

$16 - 9 =$ _____

There are _____ apples.

Independent Practice

Draw a picture to help you solve each problem.

6. There are 7 books on a shelf.
   Anna takes some books off.
   Now there are 3 books on the shelf.
   How many books does Anna take off?

   ____ − ____ = ____

   Anna takes ____ books off the shelf.

7. David has 6 pencils. Selene has 10 pencils.
   How many fewer pencils does
   David have than Selene?

   ____ − ____ = ____

   David has ____ fewer pencils than Selene.

8. Al has 5 more cars than Mike. Al has 14 cars.
   How many cars does Mike have?

   ____ − ____ = ____

   Mike has ____ cars.

Draw a picture to help you solve each problem.

9. There were 9 bikes on a bike rack.
Children rode 4 bikes away.
How many bikes are on the rack now?

_____ − _____ = _____

There are _____ bikes on the rack now.

10. Some children were playing.
Then 9 children leave.
Now there are 8 children playing.
How many children were playing at the start?

_____ − _____ = _____

_____ children were playing at the start.

MP4 11. Nikki has 14 stickers. Jason has 8 stickers.
How many fewer stickers does
Jason have than Nikki?

_____ − _____ = _____

Jason has _____ fewer stickers than Nikki.

Talk about how you can use the word *more*
to compare Nikki's and Jason's stickers.

Problem Solving: Addition of Three Numbers

Essential Question:
How do you use addition of three numbers to solve a word problem?

Words to Know
addend
sum

Guided Instruction

In this lesson you will learn how to solve word problems by adding three numbers.

Understand: What numbers and operation help you find how many in all

> Hannah has 6 oranges.
> Jack has 3 apples.
> Angela has 5 pears.
> How many fruits do they have in all?

You can add to find how many in all.

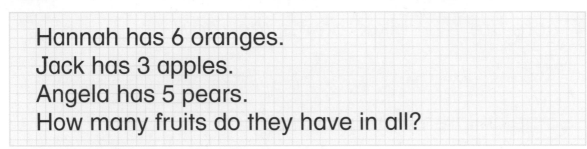

Hannah's oranges   Jack's apples   Angela's pears   fruits in all

Which numbers should you add? __6__, __3__, __5__

$6 + 3 + 5 = \blacksquare$

The three numbers you add are called addends. You want to find the total, or sum.

First add the addends 6 and 3. $6 + 3 = 9$

Then start with 9 and add the 5. $9 + 5 = 14$

$6 + 3 + 5 = 14$ The sum is 14.

▷ They have 14 fruits in all.

Guided Instruction

Understand: Solve word problems by adding three numbers

Michelle has 3 marbles.
LaTisha has 5 marbles.
Julie has 2 marbles.
How many marbles do they have in all?

Michelle's marbles	LaTisha's marbles	Julie's marbles

3   +   5   +   2   =

First add two addends. $3 + 5 = \underline{8}$

Then add the last addend
to that sum. $8 + 2 = \underline{10}$

$3 + 5 + 2 = 10$

The sum is ___10___.

➡ There are ____ marbles in all.

Guided Instruction

Connect: What you know about adding three numbers to find a missing addend

> Derrick has 5 markers. Marsha has 2 markers.
> Toby has some markers.
> They have 15 markers in all.
> How many markers does Toby have?

Step 1

Which addends do you know? __5__ and __2__

What is the sum? __15__

One addend is missing. $5 + 2 + \blacksquare = 15$

Step 2

Use counters to help you find the missing number.

Add the two addends you know. $5 + 2 =$ __7__

$$5 + 2 + \blacksquare = 15$$

$$7 + \blacksquare = 15$$

7 plus how many make 15? __8__

$$7 + \underline{\hspace{1cm}} = 15$$

$$5 + 2 + \underline{\hspace{1cm}} = 15$$

➭ Toby has __ markers.

Guided Practice

1. **Sofia has 4 stickers. Lee has 2 stickers.
Aiden also has stickers.
They have 13 stickers in all.
How many stickers does Aiden have?**

Step 1

How many stickers does Sofia have? ____

How many stickers does Lee have? ____

Sofia's stickers	Lee's stickers	Aiden's stickers	stickers in all
○○○○	○○	▪	13

$4 + 2 + ▪ = 13$

Step 2

$4 + 2 =$ ____   Draw more to make 13.

○○○○○○

$6 +$ ____ $= 13$

$4 + 2 +$ ____ $= 13$

Aiden has ____ stickers.

Think•Pair•Share

MP6 **2.** Explain how you could solve this problem using subtraction.

Independent Practice

Draw a picture to help you solve each problem.

1. A box has 2 red crayons, 5 yellow crayons, and 5 blue crayons.
   How many crayons are in the box?

   How many crayons of each color?

   red _____   yellow _____   blue _____

   Add the number of red crayons and the number of yellow crayons.

   $2 + 5 =$ _____

   Add the number of blue crayons to that sum.

   $7 + 5 =$ _____

   $2 + 5 + 5 =$ _____

   There are _____ crayons in the box.

2. Ella has 1 pink button and 4 white buttons.
   Jacob has 9 purple buttons.
   How many buttons do they have in all?

   $1 + 4 + 9 =$ _____

   They have _____ buttons in all.

Independent Practice

Draw a picture to help you solve each problem.

3. Three girls are on a bus. One more girl gets on.
   Then some boys get on.
   There are 11 children on the bus now.
   How many boys got on the bus?

   3 + 1 + _____ = 11

   _____ boys got on the bus.

4. Ethan ate 3 raisins. Then he ate 4 grapes.
   Then he ate some strawberries.
   He ate 15 pieces of fruit in all.
   How many strawberries did he eat?

   3 + 4 + _____ = 15

   Ethan ate _____ strawberries.

5. Madison has some pencils.
   Jayden has 8 pencils. Ava has 1 pencil.
   They have 18 pencils in all.
   How many pencils does Madison have?

   _____ + 8 + 1 = 18

   Madison has _____ pencils.

Independent Practice

Draw a picture to help you solve each problem.

6. Noah has 6 striped shirts. He has 2 print shirts.
He also has 5 solid shirts.
How many shirts does he have in all?

_____ + _____ + _____ = _____

Noah has _____ shirts in all.

---

7. Kate has 7 sailboats. John has 1 rowboat.
Emma has some motorboats.
They have 17 boats in all.
How many motorboats does Emma have?

_____ + _____ + _____ = _____

Emma has _____ motorboats.

---

8. Logan has some red cubes.
He gets 4 blue cubes and 5 yellow cubes.
Now he has 16 cubes.
How many red cubes does Logan have?

_____ + _____ + _____ = _____

Logan has _____ red cubes.

Independent Practice

MP6 **9.** Talk about different ways you can solve this problem. Then solve.

Matt finds 6 orange leaves.
Lily finds some red leaves.
Nick finds 3 brown leaves.
They find 14 leaves in all.
How many red leaves does Lily find?

Lily finds ____ red leaves.

MP1 **10.** Make up a problem you can solve adding 3 addends.
Draw a picture to show your problem.
Then solve the problem.

Apply Properties of Operations

Guided Instruction

In this lesson you will learn strategies that will help you add.

Understand: You can add numbers in any order

> Ken has 4 blue balloons and 5 red balloons.
> How many balloons does he have in all?

You can add numbers in any order and the sum will be the same.

Use cubes to show $4 + 5$.

Remember!
The sum is 9.
The addends are 4 and 5.

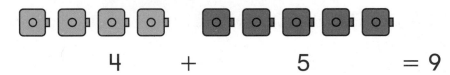

$$4 \qquad + \qquad 5 \qquad = 9$$

Now move your cubes to show $5 + 4$.

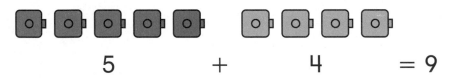

$$5 \qquad + \qquad 4 \qquad = 9$$

The sums are the same.
The order of the addends does not change the sum.

▷ Ken has 9 balloons in all.

Guided Instruction

Understand: You can add three numbers in any order

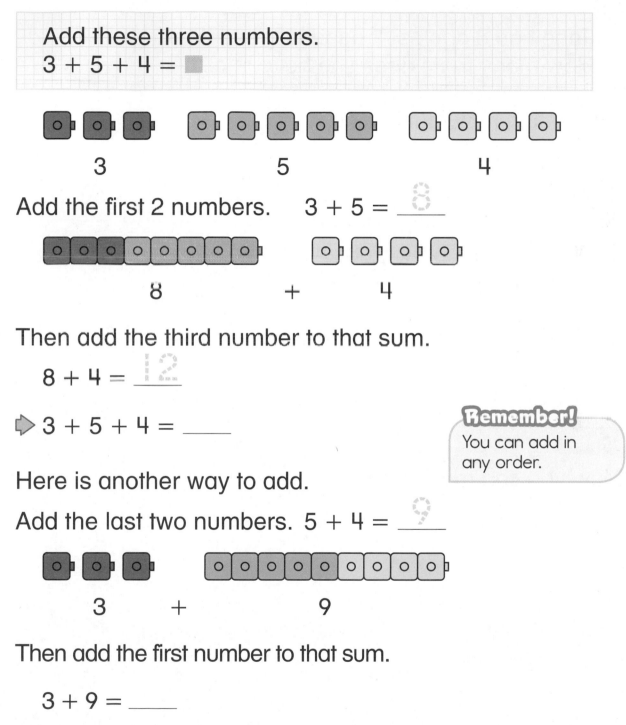

Add these three numbers.
$3 + 5 + 4 =$ ■

3   5   4

Add the first 2 numbers. $3 + 5 =$ __8__

8   +   4

Then add the third number to that sum.

$8 + 4 =$ __12__

▷ $3 + 5 + 4 =$ ____

Remember!
You can add in any order.

Here is another way to add.

Add the last two numbers. $5 + 4 =$ __9__

3   +   9

Then add the first number to that sum.

$3 + 9 =$ ____

▷ $3 + 5 + 4 =$ ____

Guided Instruction

Connect: You can group addends to help you add

> Jane has 6 apples, 2 bananas, and 4 oranges. How many fruits does she have in all?

Add to find how many in all.

$6 + 2 + 4 = \blacksquare$

Step 1

Try to make a ten by grouping the addends a different way.

$6 + 2 + 4 = \blacksquare$

$6 + 4 + 2 = \blacksquare$

Step 2

Now you can make a ten.

$6 + 4 + 2 = \blacksquare$

$\underline{} + 2 = \underline{}$

$6 + 2 + 4 = \underline{}$

▷ Jane has ____ fruits in all.

Guided Practice

1. **Add these three addends.**

   $5 + 7 + 5 = \blacksquare$

Step 1

Look at the addends.
Can you make a ten?
5 and 5 make 10.
Circle the 5 and 5 to add.

$\textcircled{5} + 7 + \textcircled{5} = \blacksquare$

Add.

$5 + 5 = \underline{\hspace{1cm}}$

Step 2

Now add the other addend to that sum.

$10 + 7 = \underline{\hspace{1cm}}$

$5 + 7 + 5 = \underline{\hspace{1cm}}$

Think·Pair·Share

MP7 2. Find each sum.

$4 + 0 = \underline{\hspace{1cm}}$ $0 + 6 = \underline{\hspace{1cm}}$ $9 + 0 = \underline{\hspace{1cm}}$

What happens when you add 0 to
any number?

Independent Practice

Show that changing the order of the addends does not change the sum.

1. $4 + 8 =$ ▨

   ____ $+$ ____ $=$ ____

   $4 + 8 =$ ____

2. $7 + 9 =$ ▨

   ____ $+$ ____ $=$ ____

   $7 + 9 =$ ____

3. $7 + 3 =$ ▨

   ____ $+$ ____ $=$ ____

   $7 + 3 =$ ____

4. $6 + 8 =$ ▨

   ____ $+$ ____ $=$ ____

   $6 + 8 =$ ____

Independent Practice

Add.

5. $6 + 2 + 3 = \blacksquare$

$6 + 2 = \underline{\hphantom{00}}$

$8 + 3 = \underline{\hphantom{00}}$

$6 + 2 + 3 = \underline{\hphantom{00}}$

6. $1 + 5 + 4 = \blacksquare$

$1 + 5 = \underline{\hphantom{00}}$

$6 + \underline{\hphantom{00}} = \underline{\hphantom{00}}$

$1 + 5 + 4 = \underline{\hphantom{00}}$

7. $2 + 4 + 5 = \blacksquare$

$2 + \underline{\hphantom{00}} = \underline{\hphantom{00}}$

$\underline{\hphantom{00}} + \underline{\hphantom{00}} = \underline{\hphantom{00}}$

$2 + 4 + 5 = \underline{\hphantom{00}}$

8. $8 + 2 + 7 = \blacksquare$

$\underline{\hphantom{00}} + \underline{\hphantom{00}} = \underline{\hphantom{00}}$

$\underline{\hphantom{00}} + \underline{\hphantom{00}} = \underline{\hphantom{00}}$

$8 + 2 + 7 = \underline{\hphantom{00}}$

9. $4 + 5 + 6 = \blacksquare$

$4 + \underline{\hphantom{00}} = \underline{\hphantom{00}}$

$\underline{\hphantom{00}} + \underline{\hphantom{00}} = \underline{\hphantom{00}}$

$4 + 5 + 6 = \underline{\hphantom{00}}$

10. $7 + 1 + 8 = \blacksquare$

$7 + \underline{\hphantom{00}} = \underline{\hphantom{00}}$

$\underline{\hphantom{00}} + \underline{\hphantom{00}} = \underline{\hphantom{00}}$

$7 + 1 + 8 = \underline{\hphantom{00}}$

Independent Practice

Make a ten.
Then add the other addend.

11. $6 + 2 + 8 =$

   $2 + 8 =$ ____

   $10 + 6 =$ ____

12. $5 + 5 + 9 =$ ▢

   $5 + 5 =$ ____

   $10 + 9 =$ ____

13. $3 + 5 + 7 =$ ▢

   $3 + 7 =$ ____

   $10 +$ ____ $=$ ____

14. $8 + 9 + 1 =$ ▢

   ____ $+$ ____ $=$ ____

   ____ $+$ ____ $=$ ____

Solve the problem. Show your work.

15. Ken had 5 gold fish. He bought 5 more gold fish and 2 angel fish. How many fish does Ken have now?

   Ken has ____ fish now.

Independent Practice

MP3 **16.** Mia and Carlos wanted to solve this addition.

$6 + 9 = \blacksquare$

Mia added $6 + 9$.
Carlos added $9 + 6$.
Who will get the correct answer? Explain.

MP1 **17.** Make up a problem for this addition example.
Draw a picture to show your problem.
Then solve your problem.

$5 + 3 + 5 = \blacksquare$

Related Addition and Subtraction Facts

Guided Instruction

In this lesson you will learn how addition and subtraction are related.

Understand: Every addition fact has a related subtraction fact

Jo has 4 marbles. Kim gives her 2 more marbles. How many marbles does Jo have now?

Start with 4 marbles. Add 2 marbles.

$$4 + 2 = 6$$

Remember!
4 and 2 are addends.
6 is the sum.

⇨ Jo has 6 marbles now.

Jo has 6 marbles. She gives 2 marbles to Kim. How many marbles does Jo have now?

Start with the 6 marbles. Take away 2 marbles.

$$6 - 2 = 4$$

⇨ Jo has 4 marbles now.

Adding to and taking from are opposite operations.

$4 + 2 = 6$ and $6 - 2 = 4$ are related facts.
They use the same numbers.

Understand: Use a related subtraction fact to find the missing addend

Mary has 9 marbles.
Four are orange and the rest are blue.
How many blue marbles does Mary have?

What number added to 4 is equal to 9?

$$4 + \blacksquare = 9$$

Use a related subtraction fact to find the missing addend.

$$9 - 5 = 4 \quad so \quad 4 + 5 = 9$$

▷ Mary has 5 blue marbles.

Remember!
4 and 5 are addends.
9 is the sum.

Understand: The unknown number is not always in the same position

Jon has 8 apples. He gives away some.
He has 3 apples left. How many apples
did he give away?

$$8 - \blacksquare = 3$$

Write the related addition fact you can use
to help you solve the problem.

$$\underline{3} + \underline{5} = \underline{8} \qquad 8 - \underline{5} = 3$$

▷ Jon gave __5__ apples away.

Unit 1 ■ Focus on Operations and Algebraic Thinking **43**

Guided Instruction

Connect: What you know about related facts

Subtract: $13 - 6 = \blacksquare$
Use a related addition fact.

Step 1

Use the two numbers in the subtraction fact to find a related addition fact.

Which number is the sum? _13_

Which number is an addend? _6_

$$\blacksquare + 6 = 13$$

Step 2

What is the missing addend in $\blacksquare + 6 = 13$?

The missing addend is _7_.

The related addition fact is $7 + 6 = 13$.
Use the related addition fact to write the subtraction fact.

▷ $13 - 6 = 7$

What related addition fact would you use to subtract?

$$14 - 8 = \blacksquare$$

$$\underline{\hphantom{00}} + \underline{\hphantom{00}} = \underline{\hphantom{00}}$$

$$14 - 8 = \underline{\hphantom{00}}$$

1. **Subtract: $15 - 9 = $** ▇
   Use a related addition fact.

Step 1

Use the two numbers in the subtraction fact to find a related addition fact.

Which number should you write as the sum? ____

Which number should you write as an addend? ____

▇ $+$ ____ $=$ ____

Step 2

Find the missing addend for the related addition fact.

____ $+ 9 = 15$

Use the related addition fact to write the subtraction fact.

$15 - 9 = $ ____

Think•Pair•Share

MP2 2. Are these addition and subtraction facts related facts? Tell why or why not.

$12 - 7 = 5$ $5 + 7 = 12$
$12 - 5 = 7$ $7 + 5 = 12$

Independent Practice

First write a related addition fact that can help you subtract. Then subtract.

1. $7 - 3 = \blacksquare$

   ____ $+ 3 = 7$

   $7 - 3 =$ ____

2. $11 - 5 = \blacksquare$

   ____ $+ 5 = 11$

   $11 - 5 =$ ____

3. $14 - 6 = \blacksquare$

   ____ $+ 6 = 14$

   $14 - 6 =$ ____

4. $16 - 8 = \blacksquare$

   $8 +$ ____ $= 16$

   $16 - 8 =$ ____

5. $10 - 4 = \blacksquare$

   ____ $+ 4 = 10$

   $10 - 4 =$ ____

6. $17 - 9 = \blacksquare$

   ____ $+ 9 = 17$

   $17 - 9 =$ ____

Independent Practice

Write a related addition fact for each subtraction fact.

7. $8 - 6 = 2$

_____ + _____ = _____

8. $12 - 8 = 4$

_____ + _____ = _____

9. $13 - 5 = 8$

_____ + _____ = _____

10. $18 - 9 = 9$

_____ + _____ = _____

Are the facts related addition and subtraction facts? Write yes or no.

11. $18 - 9 = 9$ and $9 + 9 = 18$ _____

12. $13 - 5 = 8$ and $4 + 9 = 13$ _____

13. $11 - 6 = 5$ and $5 + 6 = 11$ _____

14. $5 + 7 = 12$ and $12 - 4 = 8$ _____

Independent Practice

Circle the correct answer.

15. $12 - 7 =$ ▪   6   5   4

16. $15 - 8 =$ ▪   7   6   5

17. $6 + 7 =$ ▪   11   12   13

Add or subtract.

18. $9 - 3 =$ ____

19. $15 - 6 =$ ____

20. $8 + 5 =$ ____

21. $14 - 7 =$ ____

22. $11 - 4 =$ ____

23. $6 + 5 =$ ____

24. $17 - 8 =$ ____

25. $9 + 7 =$ ____

Independent Practice

MP8 **26.** Using the numbers 4, 7, and 11 Jeanine wrote these related addition and subtraction facts.

$$4 + 7 = 11 \qquad\qquad 7 + 4 = 11$$

$$11 - 7 = 4 \qquad\qquad 11 - 4 = 7$$

What related addition and subtraction facts can Jeanine write using the numbers 8, 5, and 13?

____ + ____ = ____   ____ + ____ = ____

____ − ____ = ____   ____ − ____ = ____

Talk about how you know that the facts are related.

MP4 **27.** Explain why you can only write one addition fact and one subtraction fact using the numbers 6, 6, and 12. Write the facts.

Relate Counting to Addition and Subtraction

Essential Question:
How can you use counting on to add or subtract?

Words to Know
count on

Guided Instruction

In this lesson you will learn how to count on to add or subtract.

Understand: You can count on to add

Alex draws 5 red circles and 2 blue circles. How many circles does he draw in all?

$5 + 2 = $ ▧

Start with 5. Count on 2.

◯◯◯◯◯ ◯◯

$5 \longrightarrow 6 \quad 7$

$5 + 2 = 7$

▷ Alex draws 7 circles in all.

Ida has 8 baseball cards. Jim gives her 4 more cards. How many baseball cards does Ida have in all? Draw a picture. Count on to solve the problem.

$8 \longrightarrow 9 \ 10 \ 11 \ 12$

Start with 8. Count on 4.

$8 + 4 = 12$

Ida has 12 baseball cards in all.

Understand: **You can count on to subtract**

Rita has 6 apples. She eats 2 apples.
How many apples are left?

$6 - 2 = \blacksquare$

Start with 2. Count on until you reach 6.

You need to count on 4 from 2 to get to 6.

$6 - 2 = \underline{}$

▷ Rita has __4__ apples left.

Miko has 9 pears.
She uses 4 pears to make some tarts.
How many pears does Miko have left?
Draw a picture to help you solve the problem.

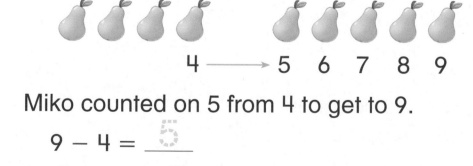

Miko counted on 5 from 4 to get to 9.

$9 - 4 = \underline{}$

▷ Miko has __5__ pears left.

Guided Instruction

Connect: Counting on and the order of addends

Use counting on to find $3 + 8 = \blacksquare$.

Start with 3. Count on 8.

$3 \longrightarrow 4 \quad 5 \quad 6 \quad 7 \quad 8 \quad \underline{\hspace{1cm}} \quad \underline{\hspace{1cm}} \quad \underline{\hspace{1cm}}$

$3 + 8 = \underline{\hspace{1cm}}$

Change the order of the addends
so you can count on fewer numbers.

$3 + 8 = 8 + 3$

Remember!
Changing the order of the addends does not change the sum.

Start with 8. Count on 3.

$8 \longrightarrow 9 \quad \underline{\hspace{1cm}} \quad \underline{\hspace{1cm}}$

$\Rightarrow 8 + 3 = 11$

Use counting on to find $10 - 7 = \blacksquare$

Start with 7. Count on until you reach 10.

$7 \longrightarrow \underline{\hspace{1cm}} \quad \underline{\hspace{1cm}} \quad \underline{\hspace{1cm}}$

$10 - 7 = \underline{\hspace{1cm}}$

Is there another way to count on
to find $10 - 7 = \blacksquare$? Explain.

Guided Practice

1. Use counting on to find 9 − 3 = .

Step 1

Start with the number you are subtracting.

What number should you start with? ____

Step 2

Count on until you reach the number you are subtracting from.

What number are you subtracting from? ____

Start at 3.

Count on.

$$3 \longrightarrow \underline{} \quad \underline{} \quad \underline{} \quad \underline{} \quad \underline{} \quad \underline{}$$

You need to count on ____ from 3 to get to 9.

9 − 3 = ____

⋎⋎ Think•Pair•Share

MP2   **2.** Talk about how you can use counting on
to find 39 + 6. What is the sum?

Independent Practice

**Count on.
Then solve.**

1. $5 + 1 = \blacksquare$

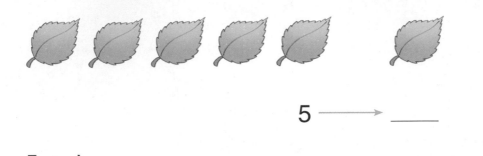

$5 \longrightarrow \underline{\hspace{1cm}}$

$5 + 1 = \underline{\hspace{1cm}}$

---

2. $7 + 3 = \blacksquare$

$7 \longrightarrow \underline{\hspace{1cm}} \; \underline{\hspace{1cm}} \; \underline{\hspace{1cm}}$

$7 + 3 = \underline{\hspace{1cm}}$

**Circle the greater addend.
Count on to add.**

3. $1 + 4 = \blacksquare$

Start at ____.

Count on ____.

$1 + 4 = \underline{\hspace{1cm}}$

4. $3 + 5 = \blacksquare$

Start at ____.

Count on ____.

$3 + 5 = \underline{\hspace{1cm}}$

Count on.
Then solve.

5. $5 - 3 =$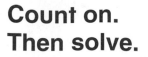

$3 \longrightarrow$ _____ _____

$5 - 3 =$ _____

6. $11 - 6 =$ ▨

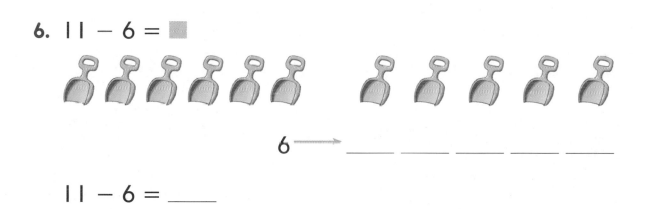

$6 \longrightarrow$ _____ _____ _____ _____ _____

$11 - 6 =$ _____

Count on to subtract.

7. $7 - 3 =$ _____

8. $10 - 8 =$ _____

9. $12 - 3 =$ _____

10. $8 - 4 =$ _____

Independent Practice

Use counting on to add.

11. $7 + 3 =$ _____

12. $9 + 5 =$ _____

13. $6 + 9 =$ _____

14. $5 + 7 =$ _____

Use counting on to subtract.

15. $8 - 3 =$ _____

16. $10 - 5 =$ _____

17. $17 - 9 =$ _____

18. $18 - 9 =$ _____

Count on to solve.

19. $2 + 4 =$ _____

20. $7 - 3 =$ _____

21. $12 - 6 =$ _____

22. $8 + 5 =$ _____

23. $7 + 8 =$ _____

24. $16 - 9 =$ _____

Independent Practice

MP4 **25.** Count on to find $6 + 8$.

Draw a picture to show how you counted on to find the answer.

$6 + 8 =$ _____

MP4 **26.** Count on to find $13 - 6$.

Draw a picture to show how you counted on to find the answer.

$13 - 6 =$ _____

Addition and Subtraction Facts to 10 (Fluency)

Essential Question:
What strategies can you use to add and subtract quickly?

Words to Know
doubles
doubles plus 1

Guided Instruction

In this lesson you will learn strategies to help you add and subtract quickly.

Understand: You can use doubles and doubles plus 1 to add

Add: $4 + 5 = $ ■

Think about doubles. $4 + 4$ is a double.

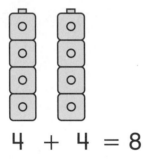

$4 + 4 = 8$

Now think about doubles plus 1.
$4 + 5$ is 1 more than $4 + 4$.
$4 + 4 = 8$, so $4 + 5$ is 1 more than 8.
$4 + 5$ is $4 + 4 + 1$.

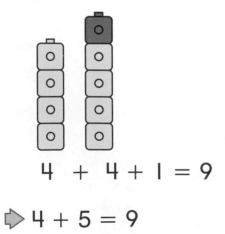

$4 + 4 + 1 = 9$

▷ $4 + 5 = 9$

Guided Instruction

Understand: You can use a related addition fact to subtract

Subtract: 7 − 2 = ■

Step 1

Find a related addition fact.

■ + 2 = 7

Remember!
Related facts use the same numbers.

Step 2

Write the missing addend for the related addition fact.

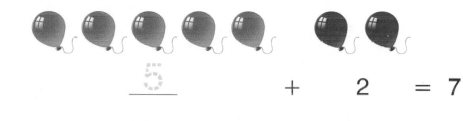

_____   +   2   = 7

The missing addend is ____.

➡ 7 − 2 = ____

Subtract: 9 − 3 = ■

Find the related addition fact: ■ + 3 = 9

Write the missing addend: ____ + 3 = 9

The missing addend is 6, so 9 − 3 = ____.

Guided Instruction

Connect: **What you know about addition and subtraction strategies**

> Rose has 10 stamps.
> She gives some stamps to Alex.
> She has 4 stamps left.
> How many stamps does Rose give to Alex?

You can subtract to find how many stamps Rose gives to Alex.

$$10 - \blacksquare = 4$$

Step 1

Choose a strategy. One strategy is to find a related addition fact.

$$4 + \blacksquare = \underline{}$$

Step 2

Write the missing addend for the related addition fact.

$$4 + \underline{6} = 10$$

The missing addend is ____.

$$10 - 6 = \underline{}$$

Remember!

4 and 6 are the addends.

10 is the sum.

➭ Rose gives ____ stamps to Alex.

Guided Practice

1. Use a related addition fact to find 9 − 6 = ■.

Step 1

Find a related addition fact.

Which number should you write as the sum? ____

Which number should you write as an addend? ____

■ + 6 = 9

Step 2

What is the missing addend for the addition fact? ____

Write the related addition fact. ____ + 6 = 9

Now write the related subtraction fact.

9 − 6 = ____

Think•Pair•Share

MP3 **2.** Write a related addition fact you would use to find 10 − 8. Then find the answer.
10 − 8 = ■

____ + 8 = ____

10 − 8 = ____

Could you use the addition fact 8 + 2 = 10 to help you find 10 − 8 = 2? Explain.

Independent Practice

Use doubles and doubles plus 1 to add.

1. $1 + 2 = $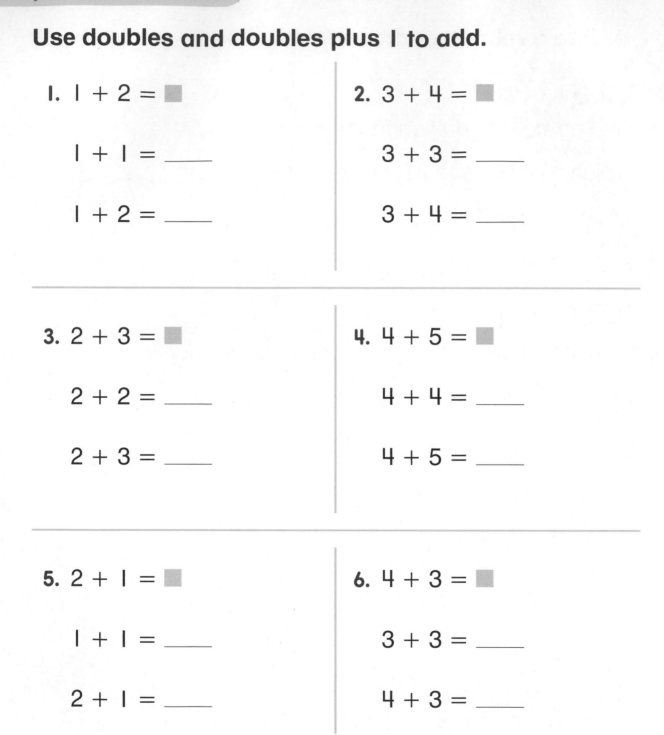

   $1 + 1 = $ _____

   $1 + 2 = $ _____

2. $3 + 4 = $

   $3 + 3 = $ _____

   $3 + 4 = $ _____

3. $2 + 3 = $

   $2 + 2 = $ _____

   $2 + 3 = $ _____

4. $4 + 5 = $

   $4 + 4 = $ _____

   $4 + 5 = $ _____

5. $2 + 1 = $

   $1 + 1 = $ _____

   $2 + 1 = $ _____

6. $4 + 3 = $

   $3 + 3 = $ _____

   $4 + 3 = $ _____

Independent Practice

First write a related addition fact that can help you subtract. Then subtract.

7. $8 - 6 = \blacksquare$

_____ $+ 6 = 8$

$8 - 6 =$ _____

8. $7 - 4 = \blacksquare$

_____ $+ 4 = 7$

$7 - 4 =$ _____

9. $9 - 5 = \blacksquare$

_____ $+ 5 = 9$

$9 - 5 =$ _____

10. $10 - 6 = \blacksquare$

_____ $+ 6 = 10$

$10 - 6 =$ _____

11. $6 - 2 = \blacksquare$

_____ $+ 2 = 6$

$6 - 2 =$ _____

12. $10 - 7 = \blacksquare$

_____ $+ 7 = 10$

$10 - 7 =$ _____

Independent Practice

Add or subtract.

13. $7 - 1 =$ _____

14. $10 - 5 =$ _____

15. $3 + 4 =$ _____

16. $8 - 4 =$ _____

17. $9 - 2 =$ _____

18. $5 + 5 =$ _____

19. $7 + 3 =$ _____

20. $6 - 3 =$ _____

Circle the correct answer.

21. $10 - 7 =$ ■   3   4   5

22. $8 - 1 =$ ■   9   8   7

23. $2 + 8 =$ ■   8   9   10

24. $6 + 2 =$ ■   7   8   9

MP4 **25.** Show how you can use doubles and
doubles plus 1 to solve this problem.
Then solve.

$4 + 3 = \blacksquare$

$4 + 3 = \underline{\hspace{2em}}$

MP3 **26.** Juan wanted to use counting on to find
$2 + 6$. He said that he could start at 2
and count on 6 more numbers to find the sum.
Larry said that Juan would have to start at 6
and count on 2 to find the sum. Who is correct?
Try both ways and talk about your answers.

Addition and Subtraction Facts to 20

Guided Instruction

In this lesson you will learn more strategies to help you add and subtract.

Understand: Making 10 to add

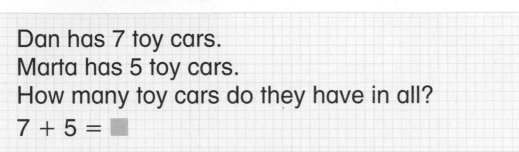

Dan has 7 toy cars.
Marta has 5 toy cars.
How many toy cars do they have in all?

$7 + 5 = \blacksquare$

Use a 10-frame and counters. Show 7 and 5.

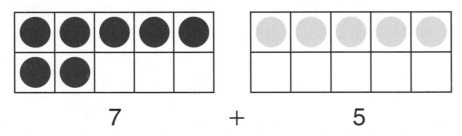

7   +   5

Move some counters over to make 10.

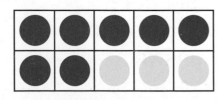

$7 + 5$ and $10 + 2$ are both names for the same number.

$10 + 2 = 12$, so $7 + 5 = 12$.

➡ Dan and Marta have 12 toy cars in all.

Understand: Making 10 to subtract

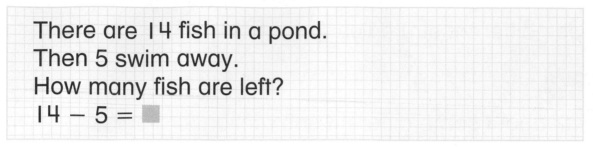

There are 14 fish in a pond.
Then 5 swim away.
How many fish are left?
14 − 5 = ■

Show 14 counters.

Take away some counters to make 10.

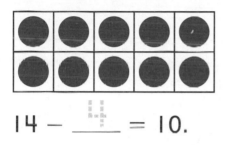

14 − ____ = 10.

You need to subtract 5. You already subtracted 4.

4 + ____ = 5, so subtract ____ more.

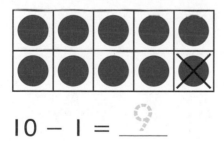

10 − 1 = ____

14 − 5 and 10 − 1 are both names
for the same number.

10 − 1 = ____, so 14 − 5 = ____.

➪ There are ____ fish left in the pond.

Guided Instruction

Connect: **Use different subtraction strategies**

Use different strategies to subtract: $12 - 8 = \blacksquare$

Step 1

Think about some different subtraction strategies.

count on   use a related addition fact   make 10

Step 2

Choose a strategy.

The problem gives the numbers 12 and 8.
You can use those numbers to find
a related addition fact.

$\underline{4} + 8 = 12$, so $12 - 8 = \underline{\hspace{1cm}}$.

▷ $12 - 8 = \underline{\hspace{1cm}}$

> **Remember!**
> Related facts use
> the same numbers.

Step 3

Choose another strategy.

You can also make 10 to find $12 - 8$.

$12 - \underline{2} = 10$

You need to subtract 8. You already subtracted 2.

$2 + \underline{6} = 8$, so subtract $\underline{6}$ more.

$10 - 6 = \underline{4}$

▷ $12 - 8 = \underline{\hspace{1cm}}$

1. Make 10 to subtract.

$16 - 9 = $ ▪

Step 1

Start with 16 counters. Take away counters to make 10.

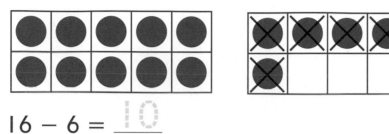

$16 - 6 = \underline{10}$

Step 2

You need to subtract 9. You already subtracted 6.

$6 + \underline{} = 9$, so subtract $\underline{}$ more.

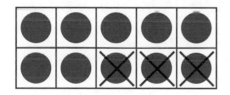 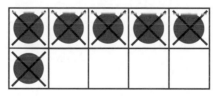

➡ $16 - 9 = \underline{}$

♕ **Think•Pair•Share**

MP3   **2.** Tell three different ways you could find $17 - 8$.

Which way do you think is best?
Explain why you chose that way.

Independent Practice

Count on to solve.

1. $9 + 3 =$ _____

2. $11 - 9 =$ _____

3. $10 - 8 =$ _____

4. $8 + 3 =$ _____

5. $8 - 5 =$ _____

6. $7 + 6 =$ _____

7. $4 + 7 =$ _____

8. $9 - 2 =$ _____

Write a related fact that can help you add or subtract. Then add or subtract.

9. $9 - 6 = \blacksquare$

_____ $+ 6 = 9$

$9 - 6 =$ _____

10. $6 + 8 = \blacksquare$

_____ $- 8 = 6$

$6 + 8 =$ _____

11. $7 + 9 = \blacksquare$

_____ $- 9 = 7$

$7 + 9 =$ _____

12. $14 - 5 = \blacksquare$

_____ $+ 5 = 14$

$14 - 5 =$ _____

Independent Practice

Make 10 to solve.

13. $9 + 4 = $ ◼

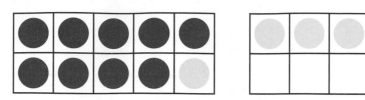

$9 + 1 = 10$

You need to add 4. You already added 1.
How many more do you need to add?

$1 + \underline{\hphantom{---}} = 4$, so you need to add $\underline{\hphantom{---}}$ more.

$10 + 3 = \underline{\hphantom{---}}$, so $9 + 4 = \underline{\hphantom{---}}$.

---

14. $8 + 5 = $ ◼

$8 + 2 = 10$

You need to add 5.
You already added 2.

$2 + \underline{\hphantom{---}} = 5$

You need to add
3 more.

$10 + 3 = \underline{\hphantom{---}}$

$8 + 5 = \underline{\hphantom{---}}$

15. $7 + 8 = $ ◼

$8 + 2 = 10$

You need to add 7.
You already added 2.

$2 + \underline{\hphantom{---}} = 7$

You need to add
5 more.

$10 + 5 = \underline{\hphantom{---}}$

$7 + 8 = \underline{\hphantom{---}}$

Independent Practice

Add or subtract.

16. $18 - 9 =$ _____   17. $11 - 2 =$ _____

18. $5 + 6 =$ _____   19. $8 - 5 =$ _____

20. $15 - 9 =$ _____   21. $9 + 8 =$ _____

22. $7 + 9 =$ _____   23. $12 - 3 =$ _____

Circle the correct answer.

24. $8 + 3 =$ ▪   11   12   13

25. $10 - 7 =$ ▪   3   4   5

26. $8 + 6 =$ ▪   12   13   14

27. $13 - 7 =$ ▪   5   6   7

Independent Practice

MP2 **28.** Explain how making 10 can help you solve $6 + 9 =$ ▪. Draw counters to help.

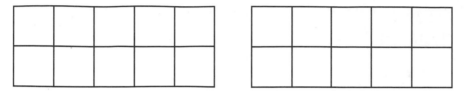

$6 + 9 =$ _____

MP2 **29.** Explain how making 10 can help you solve $15 - 8 -$ ▪. Draw counters to help.

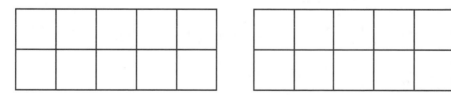

$15 - 8 =$ _____

Addition and Subtraction Equations

Essential Question:
How do you know if an equation is true or false?

Words to Know
equal sign
equation

Guided Instruction

In this lesson you will learn to tell if an equation is true or false.

Understand: Meaning of the equal sign in an addition equation

Is the addition equation true?
  $4 + 6 = 3 + 7$
Tell how you know.

A number sentence with an equal sign is called an equation.

You need to find out if $4 + 6 = 3 + 7$ is a true equation.

An equation is true if both sides of the equal sign represent the same amount.

Compare the models. Are the amounts the same?

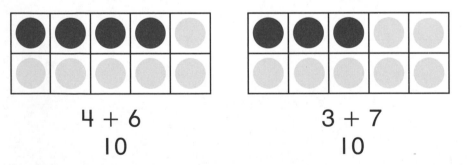

$4 + 6$ $3 + 7$
  10   10

Since $10 = 10$, both sides of the equation represent the same amounts.

So $4 + 6 = 3 + 7$ is a true equation.

Understand: Meaning of the equal sign in a subtraction equation

Is the subtraction equation true or false?
$3 = 5 - 2$
Tell how you know.

Model the amount on each side of the equal sign.

$$3 \qquad = \qquad 5 - 2$$

Compare. Are the amounts on both sides the same?

$$3 \qquad = \qquad \underline{}$$

⇨ Since $3 = 3$, the equation $3 = 5 - 2$ is _____.

Is the subtraction equation true or false?

$8 - 4 = 9 - 6$

Tell how you know.

$8 - 4 = 9 - 6$

Is 4 the same amount as 3? _____

4 is not equal to 3, so the equation is _____.

Guided Instruction

Connect: **What you know about addition and subtraction equations**

Is the equation $12 - 7 = 8 + 5$ true or false?
Tell how you know.

Step 1

Find the equal sign.

$$12 - 7 = 8 + 5$$

Remember!
An equation is true if both sides of the equal sign represent the same amount.

Step 2

Look at each side of the equation.
Add or subtract as the signs tells you to do.
Compare the amounts.

$12 - 7 = \underline{5}$ $8 + 5 = \underline{13}$

▷ Since 5 _____ equal to 13, the equation is _____.

Is the equation $14 - 7 = 2 + 5$ true or false?
Find the equal sign. Look at each side of the equation.
Add or subtract as shown.

$14 - 7 = \underline{}$ $2 + 5 = \underline{}$ $7 = 7$

Are the amounts on each side of the equation
the same? _____

The equation is _____.

Guided Practice

1. Is the equation 7 + 2 = 11 − 2 true or false? Tell how you know.

Step 1

Look at each side of the equation. Add or subtract as shown. Find the amount on each side of the equal sign. You can use cubes to help.

One side of the equation is 7 + 2. 7 + 2 = 9

The other side is 11 − 2. 11 − 2 = 9

Step 2

Compare the two answers.
Are the amounts on both sides of the equal sign

the same? _____

9 = 9, so the equation is _____.

Think•Pair•Share

MP7 **2.** Write a true equation that has both a plus sign and a minus sign.
Tell how you know the equation is true.

_____ + _____ = _____ − _____

Independent Practice

**Draw counters to model each equation.
Write *true* or *false* for each equation.**

1. 5 = 5

_____

2. 7 = 17

_____

3. 5 + 3 = 3 + 5

_____

4. 11 = 5 + 6

_____

5. 10 − 1 = 9 − 2

_____

6. 8 − 0 = 10 − 2

_____

7. 15 − 6 = 5 + 5

_____

8. 11 − 2 = 6 + 3

_____

Independent Practice

Circle the amount that makes the equation true.

9. $4 + 3 = \blacksquare$ $10 - 3$ $10 - 4$ $5 + 3$

10. $9 + 6 = \blacksquare$ $18 - 9$ $8 + 7$ $7 + 7$

11. $\blacksquare = 10 - 3$ $11 - 2$ $5 + 3$ $1 + 6$

12. $\blacksquare = 13 - 8$ $3 + 3$ $9 - 4$ $8 - 1$

Write *true* or *false* for each equation.

13. $5 + 9 = 9 + 5$ _____

14. $16 - 7 = 17 - 9$ _____

15. $14 - 8 = 5 + 1$ _____

16. $3 + 8 = 10 - 2$ _____

Independent Practice

Match to make true equations.

17. $2 + 4 =$ $8 + 5$

18. $9 + 7 =$ $4 + 2$

19. $5 + 8 =$ $6 + 8$

20. $8 + 6 =$ $7 + 9$

Write true or false for each equation.

21. $20 = 20$ 22. $7 + 4 = 11$

_____   _____

23. $5 + 3 = 5 - 3$ 24. $12 = 9 + 3$

_____   _____

25. $13 - 5 = 12 - 6$ 26. $8 + 4 = 9 + 5$

_____   _____

27. $12 - 5 = 3 + 4$ 28. $2 + 5 = 11 - 3$

_____   _____

MP7 **29.** Explain how you can make the equation true without adding.

$$9 + 7 = 7 + \blacksquare$$

Write another true equation of the same kind.

MP4 **30.** Explain how an equation can be true if it has a plus sign on one side of the equal sign and a minus sign on the other side.
Write an example.

$$\underline{\quad} + \underline{\quad} = \underline{\quad} - \underline{\quad}$$

Find Missing Numbers in Equations

Essential Question:
How can you find the missing number in an addition or subtraction equation?

Guided Instruction

In this lesson you will learn how to find the missing number in an addition or subtraction equation.

Understand: You can count on to find a missing addend or sum

Find the missing addend: $6 + \blacksquare = 11$

Start with 6. Count on to 11.

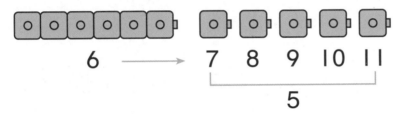

$$6 \longrightarrow 7 \quad 8 \quad 9 \quad 10 \quad 11$$
$$5$$

Count on 5 numbers to 11.
The missing addend is 5.

$\Rightarrow 6 + 5 = 11$

Understand: Use a related fact to find a missing addend or sum

Find the missing addend: $\blacksquare + 5 = 11$

Use a subtraction fact you know that has the numbers 5 and 11.

$$11 - 5 = 6$$

$\Rightarrow 6 + 5 = 11$

Remember!
Related facts use the same numbers.

Guided Instruction

Understand: You can find the missing number in a subtraction equation by counting on

Find the missing number: $12 - \blacksquare = 9$

Use counters or a drawing. Start with 12.
Group 9 together. Count on from 9 to get to 12.

$$9 \longrightarrow 10 \quad 11 \quad 12$$

$$3$$

The missing number in $12 - \blacksquare = 9$ is _3_.

▷ $12 - 3 = 9$

Understand: Use a related fact to find the missing number in a subtraction equation

Find the missing number: $\blacksquare - 4 = 9$

Use an addition fact you know that has the numbers 4 and 9.

$$9 + 4 = 13$$

▷ $13 - 4 = 9$

Remember!
Related facts use the same numbers.

Guided Instruction

Connect: **What you know about finding missing numbers**

> Hyun has some strawberries and 8 blueberries. She has 17 berries in all. How many of the berries are strawberries?

Step 1

Write an equation.

Use ■ for the number of strawberries.

$$\blacksquare + 8 = 17$$

some strawberries   blueberries   berries in all

Step 2

Think of a related fact with the numbers 8 and 17.

Find the number that makes the equation true.

$$17 - 8 = \underline{}$$

$17 - 8 = 9$ is a related fact that uses the numbers 8 and 17.

The missing number in $\blacksquare + 8 = 17$ is _____.

$$9 + 8 = 17$$

▷ Hyun has _____ strawberries.

Guided Practice

1. Find the missing number in this equation.
   ■ − 5 = 7

Step 1

Write the two numbers given in the problem.

___5___ and ___7___

Step 2

Write the related addition fact that has
the same numbers.

___7___ + _____ = _____

Is the missing number an addend or the sum? _____

7 + 5 = _____

The missing number in ■ − 5 = 7 is _____ .

_____ − 5 = 7

⋎⋎ Think•Pair•Share

MP3 **2. Write two addition facts and two subtraction facts
   using the numbers 9, 6, and 15. Talk about how
   these facts are related.**

_____ + _____ = _____   _____ + _____ = _____

_____ − _____ = _____   _____ − _____ = _____

Independent Practice

Count on to find the number that makes the equation true.

1. $9 + \blacksquare = 13$

   $9 \longrightarrow 10, 11, 12, 13$

   How many numbers did you count on? _____

   $9 + \underline{\quad} = 13$

2. $14 = \blacksquare + 8$

   $8 \longrightarrow 9, 10, 11, 12, 13, 14$

   How many numbers did you count on? _____

   $14 = \underline{\quad} + 8$

Use a related fact to find the number that makes the equation true.

3. $4 + \blacksquare = 10$

   $10 - 4 = \underline{\quad}$

   $4 + \underline{\quad} = 10$

4. $\blacksquare - 9 = 9$

   $9 + 9 = \underline{\quad}$

   $\underline{\quad} - 9 = 9$

Independent Practice

Find the number that makes the equation true. Use counters, pictures, or numbers to check your work.

5. $8 + 7 = \underline{\hspace{1cm}}$

6. $\underline{\hspace{1cm}} - 6 = 6$

7. $16 = 9 + \underline{\hspace{1cm}}$

8. $14 - \underline{\hspace{1cm}} = 6$

Independent Practice

Circle the number that makes the equation true.

9. $\blacksquare = 8 + 6$ 16   15   14

10. $\blacksquare + 2 = 8$ 7   6   5

11. $12 - 9 = \blacksquare$ 3   4   5

12. $\blacksquare - 8 = 9$ 16   17   18

Find the number to make the equation true.

13. $8 = 4 + \underline{\hphantom{xx}}$

14. $5 + \underline{\hphantom{xx}} = 12$

15. $13 - 6 = \underline{\hphantom{xx}}$

16. $\underline{\hphantom{xx}} - 5 = 6$

17. $16 = \underline{\hphantom{xx}} + 7$

18. $\underline{\hphantom{xx}} + 7 = 14$

19. $15 - \underline{\hphantom{xx}} = 7$

20. $\underline{\hphantom{xx}} - 7 = 5$

Independent Practice

MP2 **21.** Pedro has 14 stickers.
He gives some to Ella.
Now he has 8 stickers.
How many stickers does he give to Ella?

Write an equation and use it to
solve the problem.

MP3 **22.** Beth wants to find the missing number
that will make this equation true.

$9 = \blacksquare - 3$

She says that the number must be less than 9
because the related addition sentence is $3 + \blacksquare = 9$
and the sum must be greater than either addend.
Is Beth correct? Tell why or why not.

Make a ten.
Then add the other addend.

1. $7 + 1 + 9 = \blacksquare$

   $1 + 9 =$ _____

   $10 + 7 =$ _____

2. $6 + 3 + 4 = \blacksquare$

   $6 + 4 =$ _____

   $10 + 3 =$ _____

Count on to solve.

3. $1 + 7 =$ _____

4. $9 + 2 =$ _____

5. $9 - 7 =$ _____

6. $12 - 9 =$ _____

7. $8 + 5 =$ _____

8. $11 - 8 =$ _____

Write a related addition fact that can help you subtract. Then subtract.

9. $13 - 7 = \blacksquare$

   _____ $+ 7 = 13$

   $13 - 7 =$ _____

Solve each problem.
Draw a picture to help you solve the problem.

10. Matt has 4 more blocks than Jordan.
    Matt has 12 blocks.
    How many blocks does Jordan have?

    _____ − _____ = _____

    Jordan has _____ blocks.

11. Abby has 5 toys. Will has some toys.
    Jake has 8 toys. They have 15 toys in all.
    How many toys does Will have?

    $5 + \underline{\hspace{1cm}} + 8 = 15$

    Will has _____ toys.

Add or subtract.

12. $8 + 6 = \underline{\hspace{1cm}}$

13. $13 - 5 = \underline{\hspace{1cm}}$

14. $11 - 7 = \underline{\hspace{1cm}}$

15. $9 + 9 = \underline{\hspace{1cm}}$

Circle the amount that makes the equation true.

16. $5 + 5 = \blacksquare$ $\qquad$ $9 + 2$ $\qquad$ $9 + 1$ $\qquad$ $10 - 3$

17. $17 = \blacksquare$ $\qquad$ $9 + 8$ $\qquad$ $9 + 9$ $\qquad$ $7 + 9$

18. $\blacksquare - 6 = 8$ $\qquad$ 13 $\qquad$ 14 $\qquad$ 15

MP4 19. This model shows these addition and subtraction facts:

$3 + 2 = 5, 2 + 3 = 5, 5 - 2 = 3,$ and $5 - 3 = 2.$

Write all the addition and subtraction facts that this model shows.

MP2 20. How many addition and subtraction facts is it possible to write using only the three numbers 8, 8, and 16? Write these facts. How do you know you have found all the possible facts?

Progress Check

Look at how the math concepts and skills you have learned and will learn connect.

To practice your skills, go to sadlierconnect.com

KINDERGARTEN	Before Unit 2	GRADE 1	After Unit 2	GRADE 2
I Can...		**Can I ?**		**I Will...**
Count to 100 Count from a given number Write numbers from 0 to 20	☐ ☐	Count to 120 Read and write numbers to 120	☐ ☐	Count within 1,000 Skip-count by 5s, 10s, and 100s Read and write numbers to 1,000
Show numbers from 11 to 19 as ten ones and some more ones	☐	Understand place value of 2-digit numbers as tens and ones Understand 10 as ten ones	☐ ☐	Understand place value of three-digit numbers as hundreds, tens, and ones Understand 100 as ten tens
Compare numbers within 10	☐	Compare two 2-digit numbers	☐	Compare two 3-digit numbers
Add within 10	☐	Add within 100	☐	Solve word problems by adding within 100 Add within 1,000 Add within 100 to solve word problems about length Add whole-number lengths within 100 using a number line
	☐	Mentally find 10 more or 10 less than a number from 10 to 90	☐	Mentally add 10 or 100 to a number from 100 to 900 Mentally subtract 10 or 100 from a number from 100 to 900
Subtract within 10	☐	Subtract tens from tens	☐	Subtract within 1,000

HOME✦CONNECT...

In this unit your child will:

- Count to 120.
- Understand tens and ones in place value.
- Compare numbers.
- Add two-digit numbers.
- Find 10 more than and 10 less than a number.
- Subtract multiples of 10.

In first grade, your child will learn about the value of digits in a number, called place value. Your child will learn that 10 ones is equal to 1 ten. Your child will write numbers in a place-value chart to show how many tens and ones.

tens	ones
1	2

The **1** in **12** is in the tens place. It has a value of 1 ten or 10. The **2** in **12** is in the ones place. It has a value of 2 ones or 2. 12 has 1 ten and 2 ones.

Place value is a very important concept in first grade math and in all the math that will follow.

Ways to Help Your Child

Provide your child with opportunities to count. For example, a calendar is a great tool for counting. Choose a holiday or special event, and count the number of days since or until that day on the calendar with your child.

Activity: A hundred chart is a tool that will help your first grader with many concepts through the year. Make a hundred chart poster to hang in your home. Use tens and ones patterns on the hundred chart to find 10 more or 10 less than a number. For example, if you point to 29 on the chart, the number directly below it, 39, is 10 more than the number 29. The number directly above it, 19, is 10 less than the number 29.

1	2	3	4	5	6	7	8	9	10
11	12	13	14	15	16	17	18	19	20
21	22	23	24	25	26	27	28	29	30
31	32	33	34	35	36	37	38	39	40
41	42	43	44	45	46	47	48	49	50
51	52	53	54	55	56	57	58	59	60
61	62	63	64	65	66	67	68	69	70
71	72	73	74	75	76	77	78	79	80
81	82	83	84	85	86	87	88	89	90
91	92	93	94	95	96	97	98	99	100

ONLINE

For more Home Connect activities, continue online at sadlierconnect.com

Focus on Number and Operations in Base Ten

Essential Question:
How does understanding place value help you add and subtract?

Essential Question:
How can you use patterns to count on from any number to 120?

Words to Know
rows
columns
digits

Guided Instruction

In this lesson you will learn how to count to 120 starting from any number.

Understand: You can count all the objects in a group

How many flowers are there?

Count the flowers. Mark each one as you count.

⇨ There are 12 flowers.

Understand: You can count on from any number

There are 24 baseballs in a box and some baseballs outside the box.
How many baseballs are there in all?

Start at 24. Count on in order.

25 26 27 28 29 30 31 32

⇨ There are 32 baseballs in all.

Guided Instruction

Understand: Patterns in a number chart can help you count

What patterns do you see in the number chart?

1	2	3	4	5	6	7	8	9	10
11	12	13	14	15	16	17	18	19	20
21	22	23	24	25	26	27	28	29	30
31	32	33	34	35	36	37	38	39	40
41	42	43	44	45	46	47	48	49	50

Rows go across. Columns go up and down.
Use digits 1, 2, 3, 4, 5, 6, 7, 8, 9, 0 to write numbers.

Look at the red digits in the top 3 rows.
What pattern do you see?

1, 2, 3, 4, 5, _6_, _7_, _8_, _9_, _0_

Look at the first column.

What is each red digit in that column? _1_

What pattern do you see in the blue digits in
the first column?

The blue digits are in counting order from _1_ to _4_.

▷ In each row, the last digits are 1, 2, 3, 4, 5, 6, 7, 8,
9, 0. In each column, starting with row 2, the
first digits of each number are in counting order.
The last digit of each number is the same as the
red digit at the top of the column.

Guided Instruction

Connect: What you know about patterns on a number chart

What numbers do the shapes stand for?

51	52	53	54	55	56	57	58	59	60
61	62	63	64	65	●	67	68	69	70
71	72	73	74	75	76	77	78	79	80
81	♥	83	84	85	86	87	88	89	90
91	92	93	94	95	96	97	98	99	100

Step 1

To find the number that the ● stands for, start at 61 and count on.

Write the number. _66_

Step 2

To find the number that the ♥ stands for, start at 81 and count on.

Write the number. _82_

⇨ The ● stands for _66_.

The ♥ stands for _82_.

Guided Practice

1. **What number does each shape stand for?**

101	102	103	☆	105	106	107	108	109	110
▲	112	113	114	115	116	117	118	119	■

Step 1

Start at 101 and count forward to ☆.

Write the number that the ☆ stands for. _104_

Step 2

Start at 105 and count forward to ▲.

Write the number that the ▲ stands for. _____

Step 3

Start at 112 and count forward to ■.

Write the number that the ■ stands for. _____

The missing numbers are ☆ _____, ▲ _____, and ■ _____.

Think•Pair•Share

MP7 **2.** Start at 98. Write the next 5 numbers.

Talk about how you know what number is next.

98, _____, _____, _____, _____, _____

Independent Practice

Count on to find how many. Write the number. Mark each object as you count it.

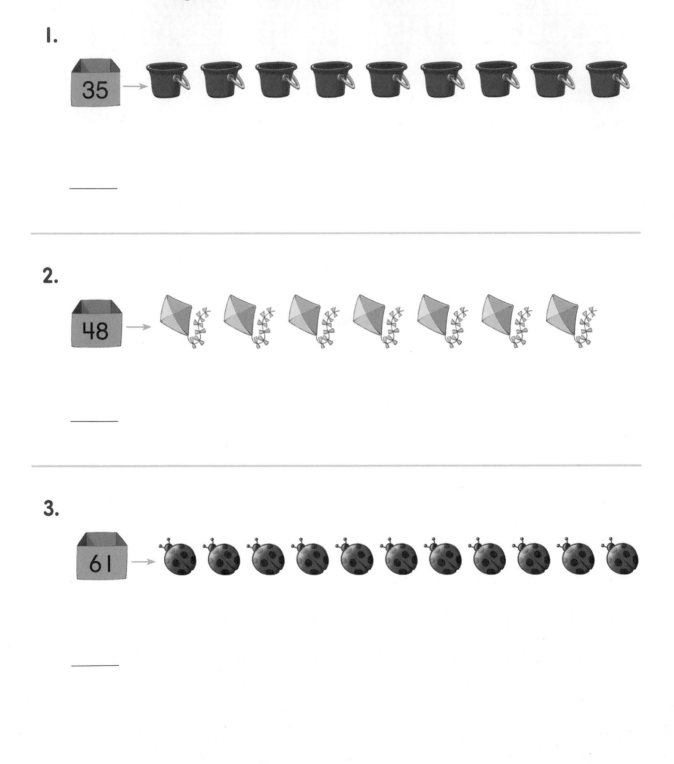

1.

35 →

_____

2.

48 →

_____

3.

61 →

_____

Independent Practice

Start at the number shown.
Write the next 5 numbers.

4. 23, _____, _____, _____, _____, _____

5. 15, _____, _____, _____, _____, _____

6. 47, _____, _____, _____, _____, _____

7. 88, _____, _____, _____, _____, _____

Circle the missing number.

8.

51	52	?	54	55	56	57	58	59	60

63   53   51

9.

?	92	93	94	95	96	97	98	99	100

81   90   91

Independent Practice

Fill in the missing numbers.

10.

1		3	4	5	6	7	8	9	
11	12	13	14	15	16	17		19	20

11.

61	62	63		65	66	67	68	69	
71	72	73	74	75	76		78	79	80

12.

	22	23	24	25	26	27	28	29	30
31	32		34	35	36	37	38		40
41	42	43	44		46	47	48	49	

13.

91		93	94	95	96	97	98	99	
	102	103	104	105		107	108	109	110
111		113	114	115	116	117			120

Independent Practice

MP8 **14.** Fill in the missing numbers on this number chart. Explain how you found the missing numbers.

1	2		4	5	6			9	10
		13	14		16	17	18	19	20
21		23	24		26	27			30
31		33		35	36	37	38		
		43	44	45	46	47			50
51	52	53			56			59	60
61	62	63	64	65	66	67			
	72			75	76	77	78	79	80
81		83	84				88	89	90
91	92	93	94	95	96			99	
		103		105	106	107	108	109	
111	112	113	114			117	118	119	

MP7 **15.** Yoki's ticket to the school show is the number that comes just before 110.
What is Yoki's ticket number?
Tell how you know.

Read and Write Numbers

Essential Question:
How can you use both numbers and words to count and to tell how many?

Words to Know
number names

Guided Instruction

In this lesson you will learn how to read and write numbers and number names.

Understand: There are different ways to show numbers

Becky sees some turtles at the zoo.
How many turtles does she see?

Say and write numbers as you count.

Number names are the words you say when you count and tell how many.

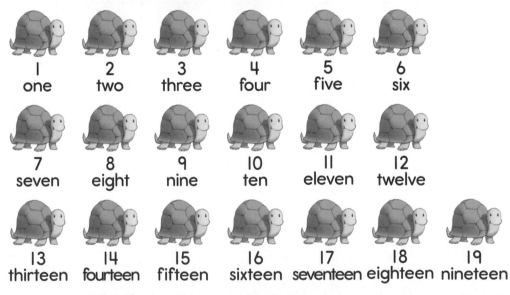

| 1 one | 2 two | 3 three | 4 four | 5 five | 6 six |

| 7 seven | 8 eight | 9 nine | 10 ten | 11 eleven | 12 twelve |

| 13 thirteen | 14 fourteen | 15 fifteen | 16 sixteen | 17 seventeen | 18 eighteen | 19 nineteen |

The last number you count tells how many turtles in all.

▷ Becky sees 19 turtles at the zoo.

Say: nineteen   Write: 19

Guided Instruction

Connect: What you know about reading and writing numbers

What are the number names for numbers from 20 to 30?

The chart shows number names for numbers that end with zero.

Use these number names and the pattern 1, 2, 3, 4, 5, 6, 7, 8, 9, 0 to read and write numbers and number names.

▷ Numbers and number names for numbers from 20 to 30 are shown below.

Number	Number Name
10	ten
20	twenty
30	thirty
40	forty
50	fifty
60	sixty
70	seventy
80	eighty
90	ninety
100	one hundred

20	twenty	21	twenty-one
22	twenty-two	23	twenty-three
24	twenty-four	25	twenty-five
26	twenty-six	27	twenty-seven
___	twenty-eight	___	___
30	thirty		

Guided Practice

1. **Use numbers and number names to tell how many marbles there are.**

Step 1

Count the marbles. Mark each one as you count.

Step 2

Write the number. _39_

Write the number name. _thirty-nine_

➡ There are _____ marbles.

There are _____ marbles.

2. Write the missing numbers and number names for numbers from 30 to 39.

30	thirty		_____	thirty-one
_____	thirty-two	33	_____	
34	_____		_____	thirty-five
36	thirty-six		_____	_____
38	_____		_____	thirty-nine

Guided Practice

3. Write the number for fifty-seven.

Step 1

Write the number for the
first part of the number name. **fifty**-seven

Step 2

Write the number for the
second part of the number name. fifty-**seven** _____

Step 3

Count on _____ from 50.

Write the number. _____

Think•Pair•Share

MP6 **4.** Sam sees 41 animals at the zoo.
Nan sees 3 more animals than Sam.
What is the number name for the number
of animals that Nan sees? Tell how you know.

_____

Independent Practice

Count. Write how many.

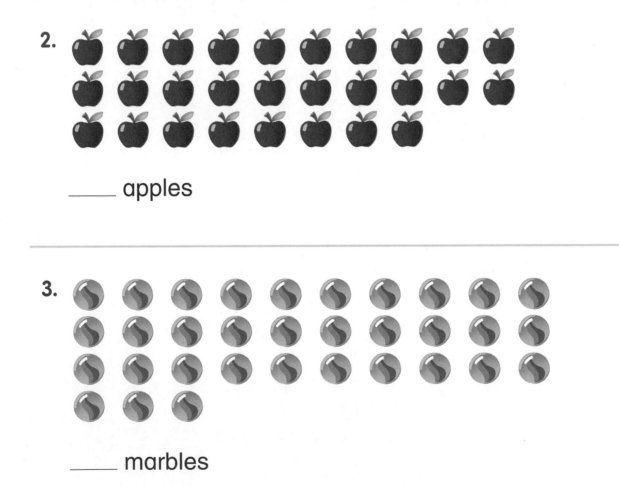

1. _____ fish

2. _____ apples

3. _____ marbles

Independent Practice

Fill in the blanks to write the number for the number name.

4. thirty-two

The first part of thirty-two is 30.

Count on ____ from ____. Thirty-two is ____.

---

5. eighty-six

The first part of eighty-six is ____.

Count on ____ from ____. Eighty-six is ____.

Read the number name.
Circle that number.

6. forty-five	55	54	45
7. seventy-six	76	70	67
8. ninety	99	90	9

Independent Practice

Draw lines to match the numbers to the number names.

9. 30   sixty-three

10. 73   thirty-eight

11. 38   seventy-three

12. 63   thirty

13. Write the missing numbers and number names.

97   ninety-seven

_____   ninety-eight

99   _____

100   one hundred

101   one hundred one

_____   _____

_____   _____

_____   _____

105   _____

Independent Practice

MP1 **14.** I am a number with 2 digits.
The first digit is two more than three.
The second digit is one less than five.
What number am I?

Write the number and the number name.
Explain how you found the number.

number _____

number name _____

MP3 **15.** Julia wants to write some number names
in counting order. She writes this list of
number names:

seventy-eight, seventy-nine, eighty-one,
eighty-two, eighty-three, eighty-four

Is Julia's list correct? Explain why or why not.

Understand Place Value: Tens and Ones

Essential Question:
How can you use tens and ones to help you understand numbers?

Words to Know
tens
ones
place-value chart

Guided Instruction

In this lesson you will learn about the value of digits in a number.

Understand: You look at the place of a digit in a number to find its value

How many tens and ones are in 15?

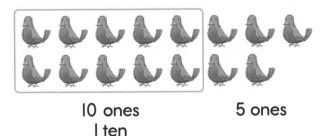

15 ones

Circle a group of 10 ones. 10 ones make 1 ten.

10 ones   5 ones
1 ten

To show how many tens and ones, you can write the number in a place-value chart.

This place-value chart shows 15.

tens	ones
1	5

The 1 in 15 is in the tens place. Its value is 1 ten, or 10. The 5 in 15 is in the ones place. Its value is 5 ones, or 5.

▷ 15 has 1 ten and 5 ones.

Guided Instruction

Connect: What you know about tens and ones

Use tens and ones to find how many counters.

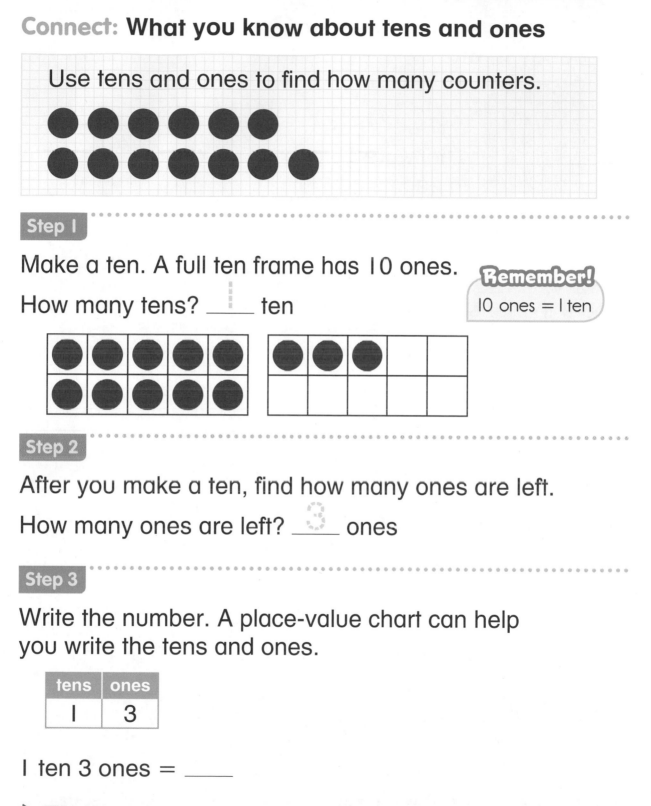

Step 1

Make a ten. A full ten frame has 10 ones.

How many tens? _____ ten

> **Remember!**
> 10 ones = 1 ten

Step 2

After you make a ten, find how many ones are left.

How many ones are left? _____ ones

Step 3

Write the number. A place-value chart can help you write the tens and ones.

tens	ones
1	3

1 ten 3 ones = _____

▷ There are _____ counters.

Guided Practice

1. Use place value to tell how many cubes in all.

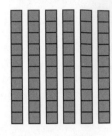

There are 10 cubes in each stack.

Step 1

A stack of cubes can stand for 1 ten.

Count the tens.

There are __6__ tens.

Count by tens. 10, 20, __30__, __40__, __50__, __60__

6 tens = __60__

Step 2

Count the ones that are left.

There are _____ ones left.

Step 3

Write the number.

tens	ones

6 tens 0 ones = _____

There are _____ cubes in all.

Guided Practice

2. **Use place value to tell how many cubes in all.**

Step 1

Count the tens. There are ___ tens.

Count by tens. ___, ___

2 tens = ___

Step 2

Count the ones that are left.

Then write the number.

There are ___ ones left.

9 ones = ___

2 tens ___ ones = ___

There are ___ cubes in all.

☆Think•Pair•Share

MP3 **3.** Write the numbers 73 and 37 in a place-value chart.

Explain how these numbers are alike and how they are different.

tens	ones

Independent Practice

Find how many tens and ones are in the number.

1. 18

Circle a group of ten.

Can you make another ten? _____

18 = _____ ten _____ ones

---

2. 21

Circle a group of ten.

Can you make another ten? _____ Circle it.

21 = _____ tens _____ one

Find how many counters.

3.

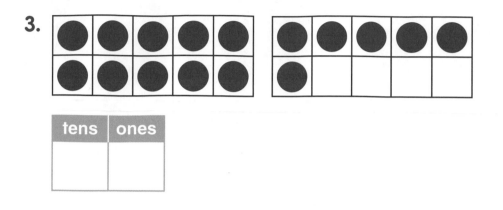

tens	ones

_____ ten _____ ones

There are _____ counters.

4.

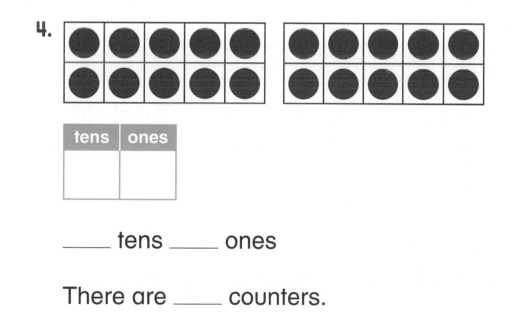

tens	ones

_____ tens _____ ones

There are _____ counters.

Independent Practice

Circle the correct answer.

5. Which number has 9 tens?   94   39   29

6. Which number has 7 ones?   73   67   76

Write how many cubes in all.

7. 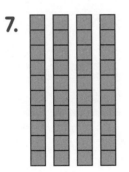   _____ tens _____ ones = _____

   There are _____ cubes in all.

8. 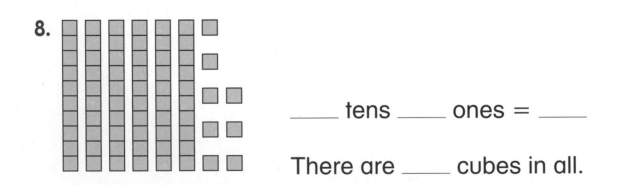   _____ tens _____ ones = _____

   There are _____ cubes in all.

Independent Practice

MP1 **9.** I am a 2-digit number with 6 ones.
I have 2 more tens than ones.
What number am I?
Draw a picture and explain how you know.

_____

MP1 **10.** I am a 2-digit number.
My tens and ones digits have a sum of 9.
My tens digit is 1 less than my ones digit.
What number am I?
Write the number in the place-value chart.
Explain how you found the number.

_____

tens	ones

Compare Numbers

Essential Question:
How can you compare numbers?

Words to Know
greater than (>)
less than (<)
equal to (=)

Guided Instruction

In this lesson you will learn how to compare numbers.

Understand: A number can be greater than, less than, or equal to another number

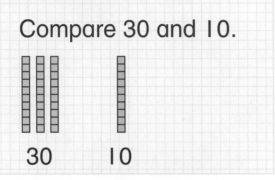

Compare 30 and 10.

30   10

Compare 20 and 40.

20   40

Compare 12 and 12.

12   12

Look at the number for each group of cubes.

▷ **>** means **greater than.**
30 is greater than 10.
$30 > 10$

▷ **<** means **less than.**
20 is less than 40.
$20 < 40$

▷ **=** means **equal to.**
12 is equal to 12.
$12 = 12$

Guided Instruction

Connect: **Use place value to compare numbers**

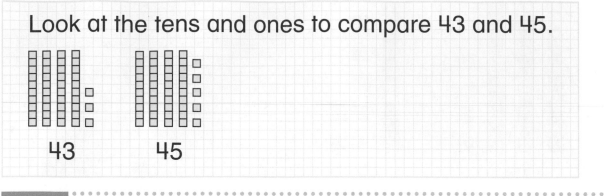

Look at the tens and ones to compare 43 and 45.

43   45

Step 1

Look at the tens place. Compare the tens.

43 has _____ tens. **4**5 has _____ tens.

The tens are the same.

If the tens are the same, you need to look at the ones to compare the numbers.

Step 2

Look at the ones place. Compare the ones.

4**3** has _____ ones. 4**5** has _____ ones.

3 is _____ less than _____ 5.

Step 3

Write *greater than, less than,* or *equal to.*

43 is _____ less than _____ 45.

➡ 43 ◯ 45

Guided Practice

1. Use place value to compare 32 and 17.

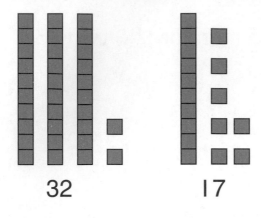

32   17

Step 1

Look at the tens place. How many tens are shown?

32 has _____ tens.

17 has _____ ten.

Step 2

Compare the tens.

3 is _____ 1.

Step 3

Compare the numbers 32 and 17.
Write *greater than, less than,* or *equal to.*

32 is _____ 17.
Write >, <, or = to compare 32 and 17.

32 ◯ 17

Guided Practice

2. Use place value to compare 26 and 29.

Step 1

Look at the tens place. Compare the tens.

26 has __2__ tens. 29 has __2__ tens.
The tens are the same.

2 is _____ 2.

If the tens are the same, you need to look at the ones to compare the numbers.

Step 2

Look at the ones place. Compare the ones.

26 has ____ ones. 29 has ____ ones.

6 is _____ 9.

Step 3

Write >, <, or = to compare 26 and 29.

26 ◯ 29

☥ Think•Pair•Share

MP1   **3.** I am a number greater than 70.
I am less than 75.
What number could I be? ____

Independent Practice

Write *greater than, less than,* or *equal to.*

1. Compare 58 and 58.

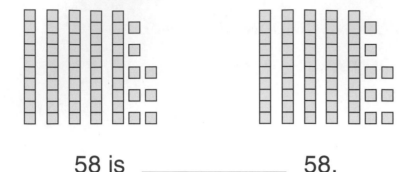

58 is _____ 58.

2. Compare 14 and 17.

14 is _____ 17.

3. Compare 63 and 35.

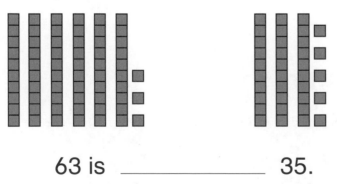

63 is _____ 35.

Independent Practice

Circle the number that is greater.

4. 71   29 | 5. 57   84

6. 63   60 | 7. 43   34

Circle the number that is less.

8. 96   99 | 9. 57   84

10. 83   60 | 11. 76   67

Compare the numbers.
Circle the correct symbol.

12. 34 ⬤ 34   >   <   =

13. 11 ⬤ 25   >   <   =

14. 78 ⬤ 72   >   <   =

Independent Practice

Compare the numbers. Write >, <, or =.

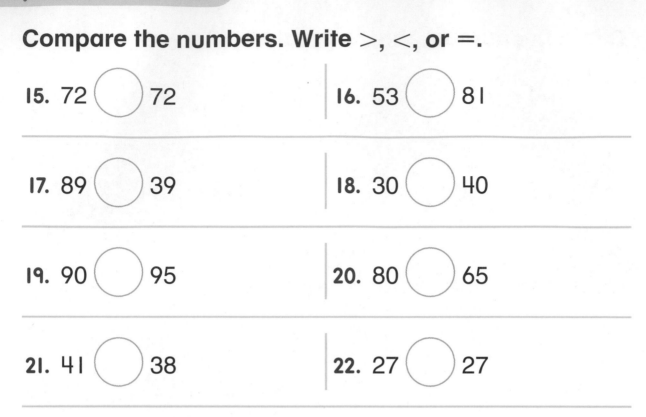

15. 72 ◯ 72   16. 53 ◯ 81

17. 89 ◯ 39   18. 30 ◯ 40

19. 90 ◯ 95   20. 80 ◯ 65

21. 41 ◯ 38   22. 27 ◯ 27

23. Amber has 117 stamps in her album.
Cindy has 109 stamps in her album.
Whose album has the greater number of stamps?

_____'s album has the greater number

of stamps because _____.

24. Juan's book has 102 pages.
Kareem's book has 111 pages.
Whose book has the greater number of pages?

_____'s book has the greater number

of pages because _____.

Independent Practice

MP7 **25.** Use each of these digits only once.

Write two 2-digit numbers.

3   5   4   8

_____   _____

Compare. Use your numbers to complete.

_____ > _____

_____ < _____

MP3 **26.** Name three numbers that are less than 40 but greater than 25.

_____   _____   _____

Write >, <, or = to compare two of your numbers.

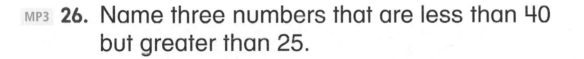

15 Add Two-Digit Numbers

Guided Instruction

In this lesson you will learn how to add two-digit numbers.

Understand: You can use models to help you add

There are 23 children on the bus. Then 5 more children get on the bus. Now how many children are on the bus?

Add to find how many. $23 + 5 = \blacksquare$

Show 23 and 5 with models.

23   5

2 tens 3 ones   0 tens 5 ones

Show 23 and 5 in a place-value chart.
Add the ones. Then add the tens.

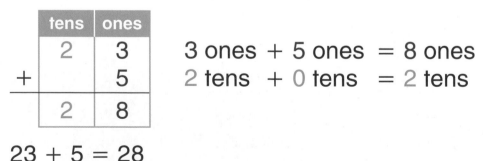

tens	ones
2	3
+	5
2	8

3 ones + 5 ones = 8 ones
2 tens + 0 tens = 2 tens

$23 + 5 = 28$

▷ There are 28 children on the bus.

Understand: **You can make a ten when you add**

> Natalie reads 36 pages. She has 7 more pages to read in the book. How many pages are in Natalie's book?

Add to find how many. $36 + 7 = \blacksquare$

Write 36 and 7 in a place-value chart.

Add the ones.

6 ones + 7 ones = __13__ ones

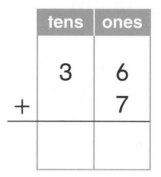

Show 36 and 7.

The models show that you can make another ten.

13 ones = __1__ ten __3__ ones

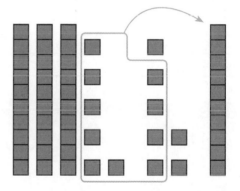

Write 3 in the ones column.
Write 1 in the tens column.

Add the tens.

3 tens + 1 ten = __4__ tens

$36 + 7 =$ ____

⇨ There are ____ pages in Natalie's book.

Guided Instruction

Connect: **You can add two-digit numbers**

Add: 54 + 30 = ■

You can use models to help you add.

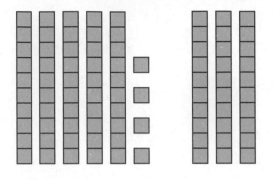

Step 1

Write the numbers in a place-value chart.
Add the ones.

4 ones + 0 ones = _____ ones

Write 4 in the ones column.

tens	ones
5	4
+ 3	0
	4

Step 2

Add the tens.

5 tens + 3 tens = _____ tens

Write 8 in the tens column.

54 + 30 = _____

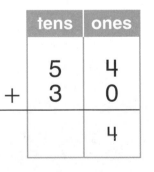

▷ 54 + 30 = ____

Guided Practice

1. **42 + 9 =** ▪

Step 1

Write the numbers in a place-value chart.
Add the ones.

2 ones + 9 ones = _____ ones

Use models to help you make another ten.

tens	ones
4	2
+	9

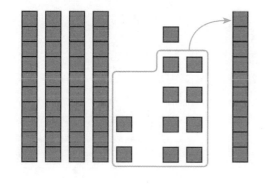

Step 2

Add the tens.

4 tens + 1 ten = ___ tens

42 + 9 = ___

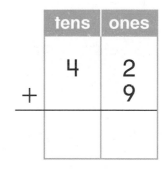

tens	ones
4	2
+	9

☺☺☺ Think•Pair•Share

MP1   **2.** When you are adding numbers in the ones place,
how can you tell if you need to make a ten?

Independent Practice

Add. Use the model and the place-value chart.

1. $64 + 3 =$ ■

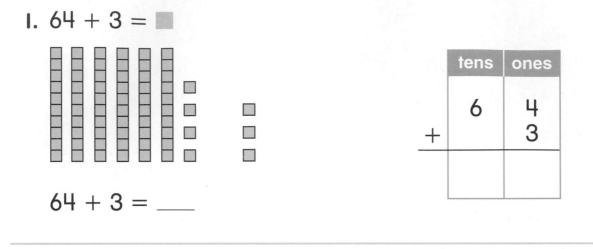

tens	ones
6	4
+	3

$64 + 3 =$ ___

2. $48 + 30 =$ ■

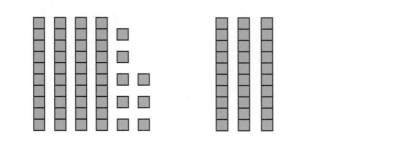

tens	ones
4	8
+ 3	0

$48 + 30 =$ ___

3. $29 + 7 =$ ■

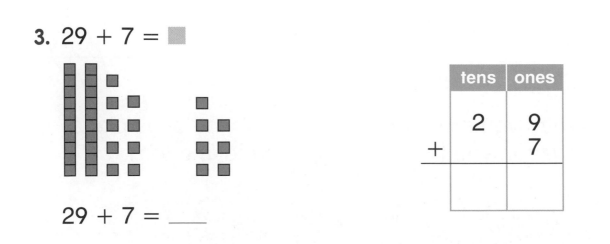

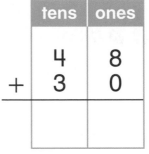

tens	ones
2	9
+	7

$29 + 7 =$ ___

Independent Practice

Add. Use the model and the place-value chart.

4. 36 + 6 =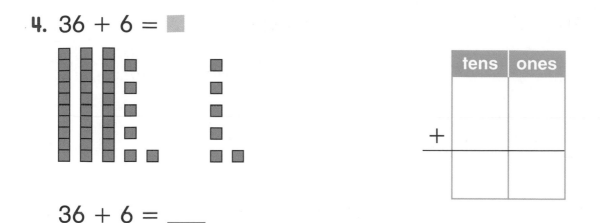

36 + 6 = ___

5. 29 + 60 =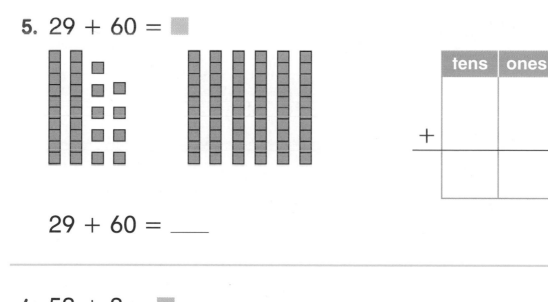

29 + 60 = ___

6. 53 + 8 =

53 + 8 = ___

Independent Practice

Add. Use the place-value chart.

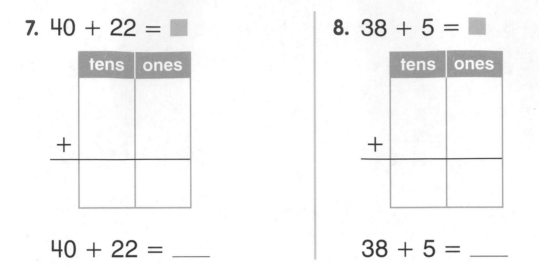

7. 40 + 22 = ▮

tens	ones
+	

40 + 22 = ____

8. 38 + 5 = ▮

tens	ones
+	

38 + 5 = ____

Add.

9. 26 + 5 = ____

10. 68 + 20 = ____

11. 13 + 50 = ____

12. 76 + 8 = ____

13. 85 + 4 = ____

14. 37 + 60 = ____

15. 39 + 8 = ____

16. 18 + 80 = ____

17. 47 + 9 = ____

18. 28 + 50 = ____

Independent Practice

MP2 **19.** Write a number between 10 and 50.
Add 9 to your number. Find the sum.
Use models or drawings to help.
Talk about how you added the numbers.

_____ + _____ = _____

MP3 **20.** A friend does not understand how to
add two-digit numbers.
Help your friend understand how to
find the sum of 27 + 40.
Use words, drawings, or models to help you.

27 + 40 = _____

Essential Question:
How can you find 10 more or 10 less than a number?

Guided Instruction

In this lesson you will learn how to find 10 more or 10 less than a number.

Understand: Find 10 more than a number

Gina has 63 beads. She needs 10 more beads to make a bracelet. How many beads does Gina need to make a bracelet?

What number is 10 more than 63?

Remember!
10 ones = 1 ten

63 = 6 tens 3 ones   To find 10 more, add 1 ten.

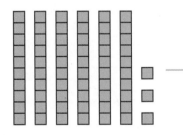

6 tens + 1 ten = 7 tens
7 tens 3 ones = 73
73 is 10 more than 63.

You can use a place-value chart to find 10 more. Look at the tens digit. 10 more is 1 more ten. The ones digit does not change.

73 is 10 more than 63.

tens	ones
6	3

tens	ones
7	3

▷ Gina needs 73 beads to make a bracelet.

Understand: **Find 10 less than a number**

Gina has 63 beads.
Mark has 10 fewer beads than Gina.
How many beads does Mark have?

What number is 10 less than 63?

63 = 6 tens 3 ones   To find 10 fewer, take away 1 ten.

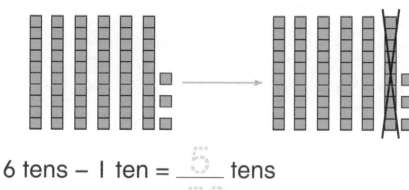

6 tens – 1 ten = ____ tens

5 tens 3 ones = ____

53 is 10 less than 63.

You can use a place-value chart
to find 10 less. Look at the tens digit.
10 less is 1 less ten.
The ones digit does not change.

53 is 10 less than 63.

tens	ones
6	3

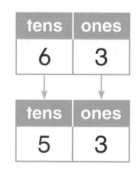

tens	ones
5	3

▷ Mark has ____ beads.

Guided Instruction

Connect: Use patterns on a number chart to find 10 more or 10 less than a number

What is 10 more and 10 less than 37?

1	2	3	4	5	6	7	8	9	10
11	12	13	14	15	16	17	18	19	20
21	22	23	24	25	26	27	28	29	30
31	32	33	34	35	36	37	38	39	40
41	42	43	44	45	46	47	48	49	50
51	52	53	54	55	56	57	58	59	60
61	62	63	64	65	66	67	68	69	70

Step 1

Find 37 on the chart. Circle it.

To find the number that is 10 more, find the number below it.

47 is below 37.

So 10 more than 37 is ____.

> **Remember!**
> When you look at each column, the number below any number is 10 more than the number.

Step 2

To find the number that is 10 less, find the number above 37.

27 is above 37.

So 10 less than 37 is ____.

⇨ ____ is 10 more than 37. ____ is 10 less than 37.

Guided Practice

1. What is 10 more and 10 less than 25?

Step 1

Find the number that is 10 less.

2 tens − 1 ten = ___1 ten___

1 ten 5 ones = ___15___

10 less than 25 is ____.

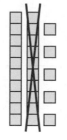

Step 2

Find the number that is 10 more than 25.

2 tens + 1 ten = ____ tens

3 ten 5 ones = ____

10 more than 25 is ____.

tens	ones
2	5

tens	ones

☟☟☟ Think•Pair•Share

MP3 **2.** Write a number between 11 and 89. ____

Find the numbers that are 10 more and 10 less than your number. Tell how you found them.

____ is 10 more.   ____ is 10 less.

Independent Practice

**Read the number in the place-value chart.
Write the number that is 10 more.**

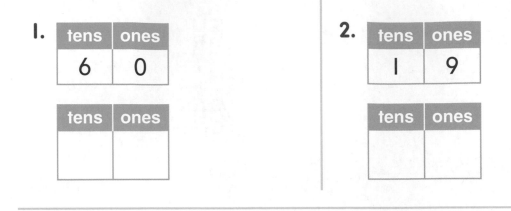

1.
tens	ones
6	0

tens	ones

2.
tens	ones
1	9

tens	ones

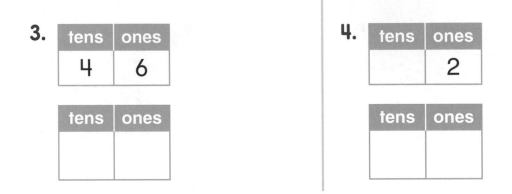

3.
tens	ones
4	6

tens	ones

4.
tens	ones
	2

tens	ones

**Read the number in the place-value chart.
Write the number that is 10 less.**

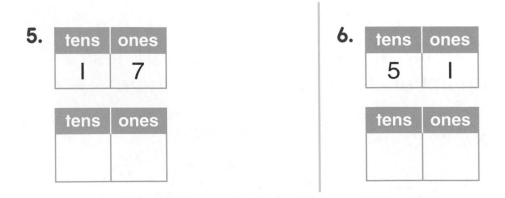

5.
tens	ones
1	7

tens	ones

6.
tens	ones
5	1

tens	ones

Independent Practice

Read the number. Write the number that is 10 more and 10 less. Draw models to check your answer.

7. 24

10 more than 24 is _____.

10 less than 24 is _____.

8. 53

10 more than 53 is _____.

10 less than 53 is _____.

9. 87

10 more than 87 is _____.

10 less than 87 is _____.

10. 18

10 more than 18 is _____.

10 less than 18 is _____.

Independent Practice

**Each puzzle below is part of a number chart.
Fill in the missing numbers.**

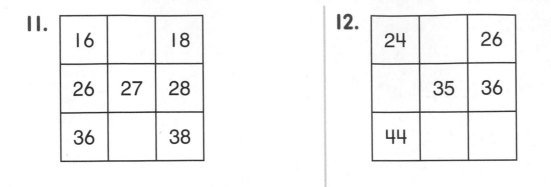

11.

16		18
26	27	28
36		38

12.

24		26
	35	36
44		

---

13. Bonnie's toy chest has 23 toys in it.
The toy chest has room for 10 more toys.
How many toys can fit in Bonnie's toy chest?

_____ toys can fit in Bonnie's toy chest.

---

14. Rudy wanted to bring 24 peaches to a party.
When he opened the bag, he found he had
10 fewer peaches than he thought. How many
peaches did he find in the bag?

Rudy found _____ peaches in the bag.

Independent Practice

MP7 **15.** Meg wrote a mystery number.
She gave this clue:
69 is 10 more than my number.
What is her mystery number?
What is 10 less than her number?
Tell how you found her mystery number.

Mystery number: _____

_____ is 10 less than her mystery number.

MP8 **16.** Fill in the missing numbers on this number chart puzzle piece. Talk about how you found the missing numbers.

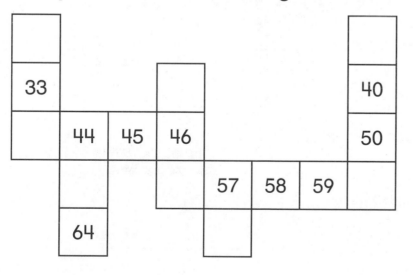

Essential Question:
How can you subtract tens from tens?

Guided Instruction

In this lesson you will learn how to subtract tens from tens.

Understand: Use place-value models and a place-value chart to help you subtract tens from tens

A clown wants to blow up 40 balloons. He blows up 10 balloons. How many more balloons does he need to blow up?

Subtract to find how many more. $40 - 10 = $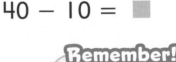

Use place-value models.

Remember!
10 ones = 1 ten

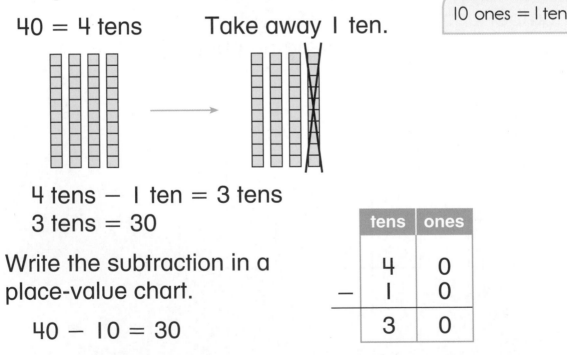

$40 = 4$ tens   Take away 1 ten.

4 tens − 1 ten = 3 tens
3 tens = 30

Write the subtraction in a place-value chart.

$40 - 10 = 30$

tens	ones
4	0
− 1	0
3	0

➡ The clown needs to blow up 30 more balloons.

Guided Instruction

Connect: Use what you know about place value and subtraction facts

Paul has 50 pencils. He gives 30 pencils to Marla. How many pencils does Paul have left?

Subtract to find how many are left.   50 − 30 = ■

Step 1

Think about how many tens are in each number.

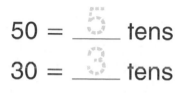

50 = ___5___ tens

30 = ___3___ tens

Step 2

Think of a subtraction fact that uses the tens digit of each number.

5 − 3 = ____

Step 3

Subtract the tens.
Write the tens as two-digit numbers.

5 tens − 3 tens = ___2___ tens

50   −   30   =   20

▷ Paul has ____ pencils left.

Guided Practice

1. **Use the patterns in the chart to help you subtract: 80 − 20 = ▇.**

Remember!
Every number on the chart is 10 less than the number just below it.

Step 1

Find 80 on the chart. Circle it.

1	2	3	4	5	6	7	8	9	10
11	12	13	14	15	16	17	18	19	20
21	22	23	24	25	26	27	28	29	30
31	32	33	34	35	36	37	38	39	40
41	42	43	44	45	46	47	48	49	50
51	52	53	54	55	56	57	58	59	60
61	62	63	64	65	66	67	68	69	70
71	72	73	74	75	76	77	78	79	(80)
81	82	83	84	85	86	87	88	89	90
91	92	93	94	95	96	97	98	99	100

Step 2

To subtract 20, think: 20 = __2__ tens

Every time you move up a number in a column, you subtract 10.

To subtract 20, you have to move up ____ numbers on the hundred chart.

Start at 80. Move up two numbers.

__70__ is 10 less than 80, so ____ is 20 less than 80.

80 − 20 = ____

Guided Practice

2. **90 − 50 = ▪**

Step 1

Think about how many tens are in each number.

90 = ____ tens   50 = ____ tens

Step 2

Write a subtraction fact using the tens
digits in 90 and 50. Use it to solve the problem.

9 − 5 = ____

90 − 50 = ____

☝ Think•Pair•Share

MP7   3. Choose one of these numbers: 50, 60, 70, 80, 90.
Subtract 40 from that number.

____ − 40 = ____

Choose a different number from the list.
Subtract 40 from that number.

____ − 40 = ____

Talk about how the subtractions are alike and
how they are different.

Independent Practice

Use the models to help you subtract.

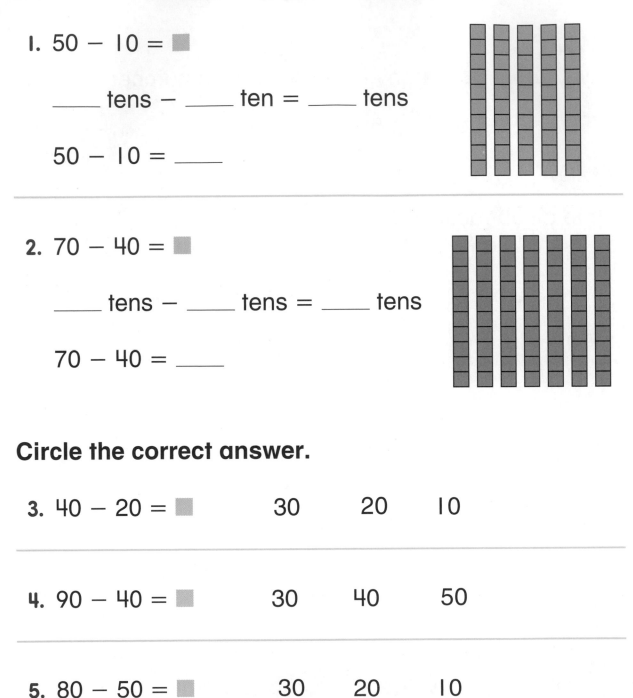

1. $50 - 10 = \blacksquare$

   _____ tens − _____ ten = _____ tens

   $50 - 10 = $ _____

2. $70 - 40 = \blacksquare$

   _____ tens − _____ tens = _____ tens

   $70 - 40 = $ _____

Circle the correct answer.

3. $40 - 20 = \blacksquare$ 30   20   10

4. $90 - 40 = \blacksquare$ 30   40   50

5. $80 - 50 = \blacksquare$ 30   20   10

Independent Practice

Subtract.

6. 60 − 60 = _____

7. 90 − 70 = _____

8. 40 − 30 = _____

9. 80 − 30 = _____

10. 70 − 40 = _____

11. 60 − 40 = _____

12. 70 − 70 = _____

13. 80 − 20 = _____

14. 90 − 80 = _____

15. 70 − 20 = _____

Independent Practice

Each puzzle piece below is part of a hundred chart.

Fill in the missing numbers.

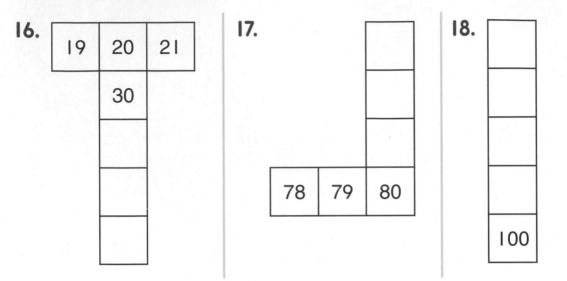

16.

19	20	21
	30	

17.

| 78 | 79 | 80 |

18.

100

Solve each problem. Show your work.

19. Ava has 70 stamps.
    She gives away 30 stamps.
    How many stamps does
    she have left?

    Ava has ____ stamps left.

20. A store has 80 boxes of crayons.
    The store sells 60 boxes of crayons.
    How many boxes of crayons are left?

    There are ____ boxes of crayons left.

Independent Practice

MP1 **21.** Celia wrote the number 60.
She said this was her answer when she
subtracted 30 from her number.
What was her number?
Tell how you found her number.

Her number was _____.

_____

MP8 **22.** Raj says he can subtract 5 tens from his
secret number on the hundred chart.
The answer will be 20.
What is Raj's secret number?

_____

_____

MP3 **23.** Joan says that the number that is
2 tens less than 90 is the same as
the number that is 3 tens less than 80.
Is Joan correct? Talk about why or why not.

_____

1. Count on to find how many. Write the number.
   Mark each object as you count it.

_____

---

2. Fill in the missing numbers.

	82	83	84	85	86	87		89	90
91	92	93	94	95		97	98	99	
101	102	103			106	107	108		110
111				115	116		118		

Read the number name. Circle that number.

3. fifty-two   42   43   52

Compare the numbers. Write <, =, or >.

4. 43 ◯ 36   5. 70 ◯ 80

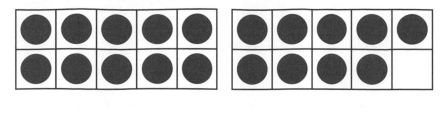

6. Find how many counters.

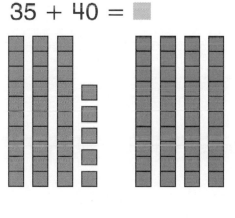

_____ ten   _____ ones

There are _____ counters.

---

7. Add.

35 + 40 = ■

35 + 40 = _____

---

8. Subtract.
Draw models to show your answer.

90 − 30 = ■

90 − 30 = _____

MP1 **9.** I am a 2-digit number.
My tens and ones digits have a sum of 10.
I have 2 more tens than ones.
What number am I?

Write the number in the place-value chart.
Explain how you found the number.

_____

tens	ones

MP7 **10.** Cole wrote a mystery number.
He gave this clue: 47 is 10 more than my number.
What is his mystery number?

Mystery number: _____

What is 10 less than his mystery number?

_____ is 10 less than his mystery number.

Tell how you found his mystery number.

Performance Tasks

Performance Tasks show your understanding of the math that you have learned.

Beginning This Task

This is the beginning of a Performance Task. The next three pages have problems for you to solve.

As you work, you will:

1. Show that you can use math skills and concepts.

2. Decide how to solve a problem.

3. Use different ways to model and solve real-world problems.

Tips to help you!

- Read each problem carefully.
- Plan how you will solve the problem.
- Check your work.
- Be ready to show your work or explain your thinking.

Performance Task I

Playground Time

I. Mrs. Bell's class is on the playground.
There are 11 children playing on the swings.
6 of the children on the swings are girls.
How many children on the swings are boys?

a. Write an equation that can help you solve the problem. Use a ? to stand for the unknown number. Write + or − in the ◯.

____ ◯ ____ = ____

b. Write another equation using a different operation you can use to solve the problem. Use a ? to stand for the unknown number. Write + or − in the ◯.

____ ◯ ____ = ____

c. How many children on the swings are boys?

There are ____ boys on the swings.

d. Does it matter which equation you use to solve? Explain.

Recycle Time

2. Deborah picks up 28 bottles.
She puts them in the recycle bin.
After lunch, she picks up 6 more bottles.

   a. Draw the bottles that Deborah picked up
   after lunch.

   Recycle bin
   28 bottles   _____ _____ _____ _____ _____ _____

   b. Start at 28. Count on. Say and write the
   number below the bottles you drew for 2a.

   c. How many bottles did Deborah pick up in all?

   _____ bottles

   d. Write the number name for the total.

   _____ bottles

Sticker Books

3. Hector and Jess collect stickers.
   Hector has 20 stickers.
   Jess has 40 stickers.

   a. Compare the number of stickers each child
      has. Use <, =, or >.

      _____ ◯ _____

   b. Hector gets 10 more stickers.
      How many stickers does Hector have now?

      _____ stickers

   c. Jess gives away 20 of her stickers.
      How many stickers does Jess have left?
      Draw a picture to check your answer.

      _____ stickers

Progress Check

Unit 3

Look at how the math concepts and skills you have learned and will learn connect.

To practice your skills, go to sadlierconnect.com.

KINDERGARTEN		GRADE 1		GRADE 2
I Can...	Before Unit 3	**Can I ?**	After Unit 3	**I Will...**
Understand length Compare lengths	☐	Compare and order objects by length	☐	Measure to compare lengths
	☐	Measure length in length units	☐	Use appropriate tools to measure length Measure the length of an object with two different units Estimate lengths in inches, feet, centimeters, and meters
	☐	Tell and write time to the hour and half-hour	☐	Tell and write time to the nearest five minutes
Classify objects into categories Count how many in each category Compare sorted groups	☐ ☐	Show data in charts and tables Compare data in charts and tables	☐ ☐	Show length measurements on a line plot Draw a picture graph and a bar graph for the same data Solve problems using data shown in a bar graph

HOME◆CONNECT...

In this unit your child will:

- Compare and order lengths.
- Measure length in length units.
- Tell time on the hour and half hour.
- Learn the value of coins (Optional)
- Use tables.

Ways to Help Your Child

Playing games with your child is a wonderful way to practice math skills. Board games and card games that use counting are a fun way to help your child build his or her skills.

Look for opportunities to emphasize the importance of measurement and data in daily life. Understanding the news, reading a magazine article, and evaluating the truth of a TV ad often require knowing about data and how to interpret it. When working on home repairs, cooking, sewing, building, planting, or following a hobby—the ability to successfully complete a project can depend on the ability to measure accurately.

An exciting concept that your child will learn in first grade is how to tell time by reading both an analog and a digital clock. In this unit, your child will learn how to tell time to the hour and to the half hour.

You can ask your child to help tell time at home. Make note of the hour and half-hour times that you begin or end activities, like starting sports practice, eating dinner, or reading a book.

Activity: In this unit, your child will learn to measure the length of objects using shorter objects called length units. For example, they will measure the length of a piece of ribbon using paper clips as the length unit. They will place paper clips end to end with no gaps or overlap and record the length by writing how many paper clips long the object is. Provide your child with paper clips or choose some other length unit. Ask him or her to measure the length of objects in your home such as the length of a table, the width of a chair, and so on.

ONLINE

For more Home Connect activities, continue online at sadlierconnect.com

Focus on Measurement and Data

Essential Question:
How can you tell what time it is?

18 Compare and Order Lengths

Essential Question:
How can you compare and order the lengths of objects?

Words to Know
length

Guided Instruction

In this lesson you will learn how to compare and order the lengths of objects.

Understand: Comparing the lengths of objects

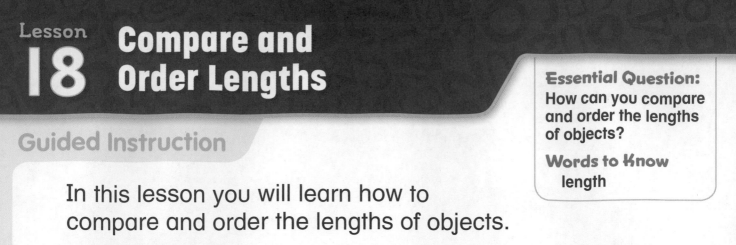

Which is longer? Which is shorter?

Compare the length of the paintbrush and the length of the marker.

Line up the left ends of the objects.

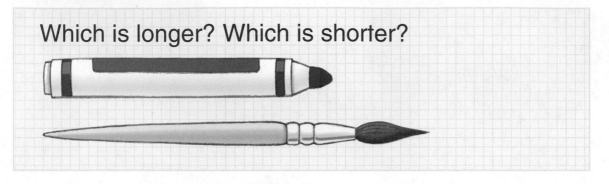

The right end of the paintbrush is farther from the line, so it is longer.

The right end of the marker is closer to the line, so it is shorter.

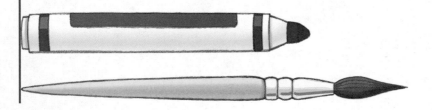 The paintbrush is longer than the marker.
The marker is shorter than the paintbrush.

Understand: **Ordering objects by length**

Order these objects from shortest to longest.

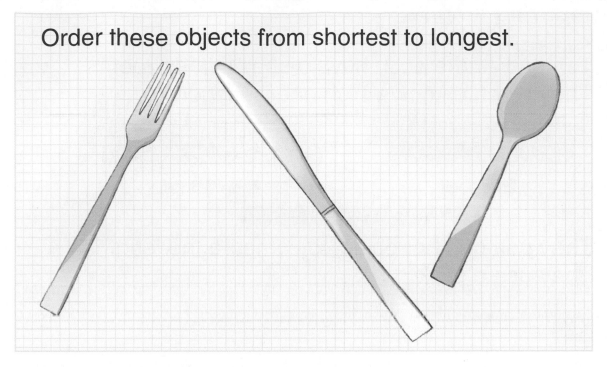

Line up the left ends of the objects.

Compare.

The _____spoon_____ is the shortest.

The _____knife_____ is the longest.

➡ The order from shortest to longest is

_____ , _____ , _____ .

Guided Instruction

Connect: **Use what you know about comparing lengths**

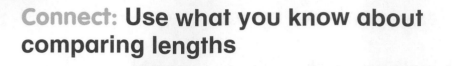

Tim and Andre each have a shelf in their room. They want to know which one is longer.

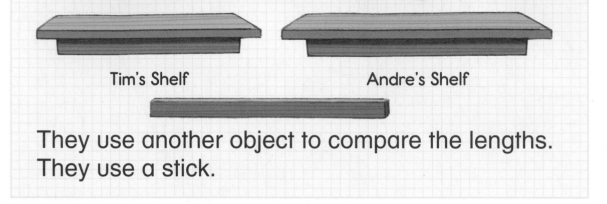

Tim's Shelf   Andre's Shelf

They use another object to compare the lengths. They use a stick.

Step 1

Compare Tim's shelf to the stick.

Tim's shelf is _____shorter_____ than the stick.

Step 2

Compare Andre's shelf to the stick.

Andre's shelf is _____longer_____ than the stick.

▷ Andre's shelf is _____ than Tim's shelf.

MP3 **8.** Sam says the crayon is longer than the scissors.
Do you agree with Sam? Tell why or why not.

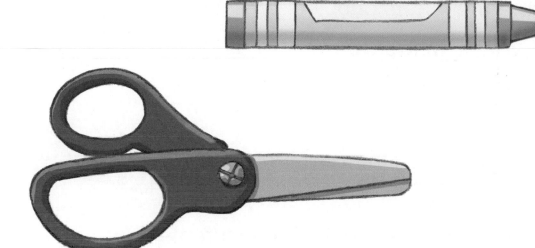

MP6 **9.** Find three objects in the classroom.
Put them in order from shortest to longest.
Explain how you put them in order.

Measure with Same-Size Length Units

Essential Question:
How can you measure the length of objects?

Words to Know
  unit

Guided Instruction

In this lesson you will learn how to measure the length of objects.

Understand: Measure objects using other objects

How long is the pencil?

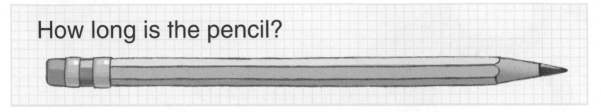

Use a paper clip as a unit of measurement.

Place a paper clip at one end of the pencil.

Add paper clips one at a time.

Make sure they touch but do not overlap.

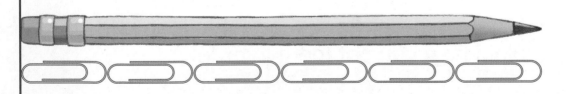

Stop when you get to the end of the pencil.

Count how many paper clips you used.

▷ The pencil is 6 paper clips long.

Understand: Use different units to measure

How long is the marker?

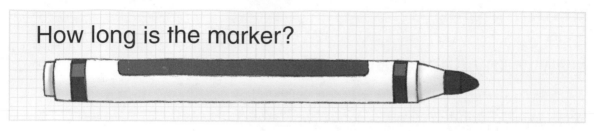

Line up paper clips above the marker.

Count the paper clips.

Remember!
Make sure the units do not overlap.

The marker is _____ paper clips long.

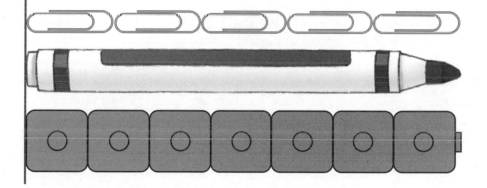

Line up cubes below the marker.

Count the cubes.

The marker is _____ cubes long.

▷ Different units give you different measurements.

The marker is _____ paper clips long

and it is _____ cubes long.

Guided Instruction

Connect: What you know about measuring length

How many cubes long is the crayon?

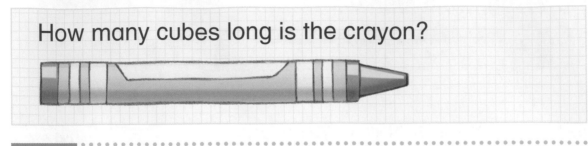

Step 1

Check that the cubes start at one end of the crayon.

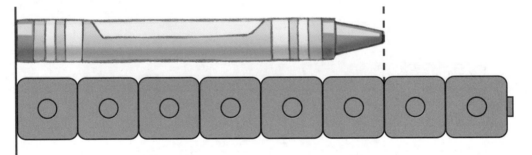

Step 2

Find where the crayon ends.

Step 3

Count how many cubes are between the two ends of the crayon.

There are ___ cubes.

▷ The crayon is ___ cubes long.

1. **How long is the feather?**

| Step 1 |

Start at one end. Line up paper clips one by one.
Make sure they do not overlap.

| Step 2 |

Count how many paper clips there are.

There are _____ paper clips.

The feather is _____ paper clips long.

Think•Pair•Share

MP3 2. Clay and Alli use paper clips to measure
a pencil case.

Clay uses large paper clips.
Alli uses small paper clips.
Will they get the same measurement?
If not, who will get a greater number? Explain.

Independent Practice

How long is each object?

I.

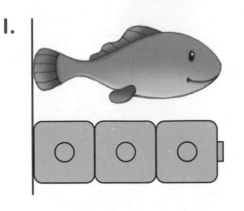

_____ cubes

2.

_____ paper clips

3.

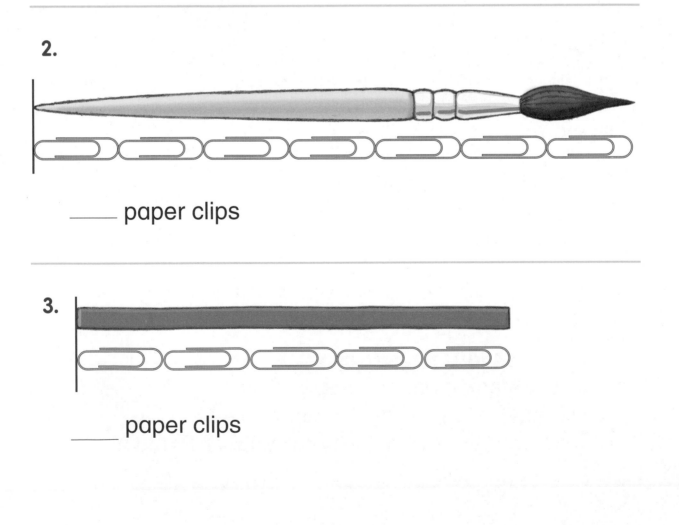

_____ paper clips

Independent Practice

How long is each object?

4.

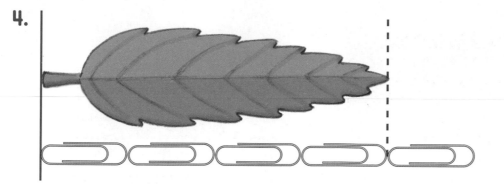

_____ paper clips

5.

_____ cubes

Independent Practice

Circle the correct measurement.

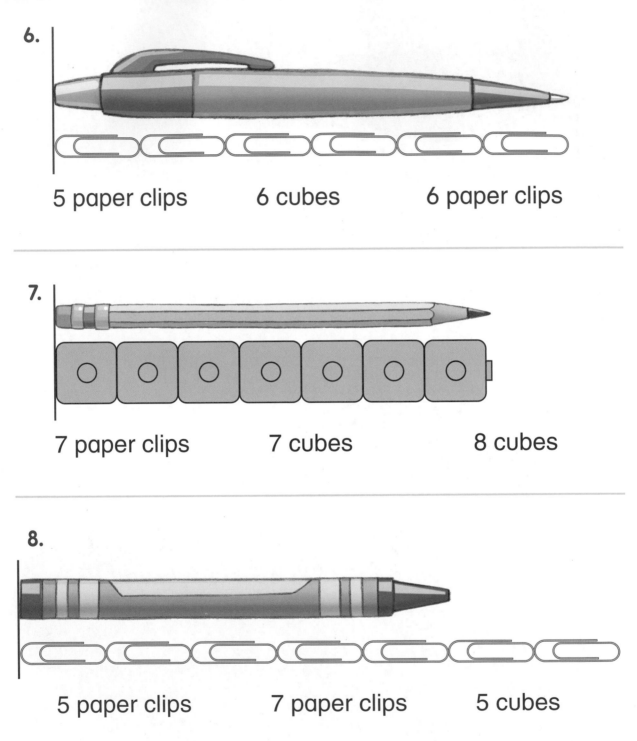

6.

5 paper clips   6 cubes   6 paper clips

7.

7 paper clips   7 cubes   8 cubes

8.

5 paper clips   7 paper clips   5 cubes

Independent Practice

MP6 **9.** Sue, Brandon, and Ana measured a straw.

Sue says the straw is 10 paper clips long.

Brandon says the straw is 6 paper clips long.

Ana says the straw is 7 paper clips long.

Who has the correct measurement?
Talk about why the others do not.

Essential Question:
How can you tell time?

Words to Know
 clock
 hour hand
 hour
 minute hand
 minutes
 half hour

Guided Instruction

In this lesson you will learn how to tell time.

Understand: **Tell time to the hour**

Nathan is going to a movie. The clock shows the time that the movie starts.

What time does the movie start?

Use the hands on a clock to tell time.

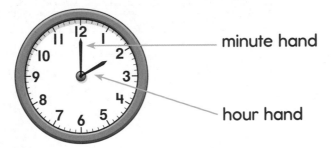

minute hand

hour hand

The shorter hand is the hour hand. It points to the hour. The hour hand points to 2.

The longer hand is the minute hand.

When the minute hand points to 12, no minutes have passed the hour, so you say o'clock.

Read the time: two o'clock
Write the time: 2:00

➡️ The movie starts at two o'clock, or 2:00.

Guided Instruction

Understand: **Tell time to the half hour**

The clock shows the time Amber's music class starts. What time does her music class start?

> **Remember!**
> The minute hand is the longer hand. The hour hand is the shorter hand.

The hour hand is between 4 and 5.
The time is between 4 o'clock and 5 o'clock.

The minute hand points to __6__.
When the minute hand points to 6, it is halfway around the clock.

There are 60 minutes in one hour.
There are 30 minutes in a half hour.

The time is 30 minutes **past** 4 o'clock.

Read the time: _four thirty_

Write the time: _4_ : _30_

▷ Amber's music class starts at ____:____.
   4:30 is also 30 minutes **before** 5 o'clock.

Guided Instruction

Connect: What you know about telling time and using a digital clock

You know how to read the time shown by clock hands. The time shown on the clock below is 10:00.

A digital clock does not have clock hands. Read and write the time shown on the digital clock below.

hour minutes

Step 1

What is the hour? __10__

Step 2

How many minutes have passed? __0__

Read the time as __ten__ o'clock.

Write the time as ____:____.

▷ The time on the digital clock is _____ o'clock,

or ____:____.

1. **What time is it?**

Step 1

Look at the hour hand.

The hour hand is between ___9___ and ___10___.

The time is past ____ o'clock.

Step 2

Look at the minute hand.

The minute hand is pointing to ____.

How many minutes after the hour is it? ____

The time is ____:____.

☆ Think•Pair•Share

MP5   2. Read the time on the
   digital clock.

   Draw the hands on the clock
   to show the same time.
   Tell how you know where to
   draw the hands.

Independent Practice

Write the time.

1.

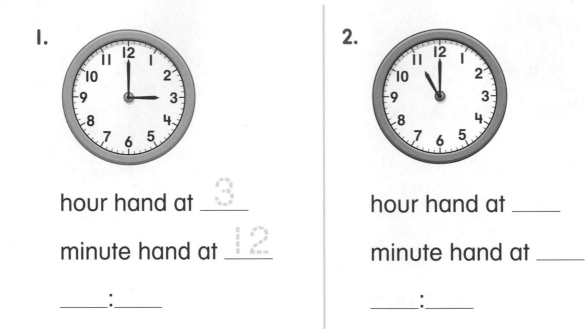

hour hand at __3__

minute hand at __12__

____:____

2.

hour hand at ____

minute hand at ____

____:____

3.

hour hand between

__2__ and __3__

minute hand at __6__

____:____

4.

hour hand between

____ and ____

minute hand at ____

____:____

Independent Practice

MP1 **13.** Louis draws the hour hand on the clock between the 1 and the 2. Then he draws a minute hand pointing to the 6.

What time does his clock show? Draw hands on the clock to help. Talk about how you found the time.

_____ : _____

MP4 **14.** Find the mystery time.
It is 30 minutes past the hour.
The hour hand is between 5 and 6.

Draw the hands on the clock.
Explain how you found the mystery time.

_____ : _____

Essential Question:
How do you find the value of a group of coins?

Guided Instruction

In this lesson you will learn about coins and their values.

Understand: Identify coins and compare their values

Words to Know
penny
cent
nickel
dime
quarter

penny	nickel	dime	quarter

1¢	5¢	10¢	25¢
1 cent	5 cents	10 cents	25 cents

Jamie has these two coins. Which coin is worth more?

This is a dime.
It is worth 10 cents.

This is a __nickel__.

It is worth __5__ cents.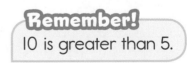

10 cents is more than 5 cents.

> The __dime__ is worth more than the __nickel__.

Remember!
10 is greater than 5.

Understand: Count on and add to find the value of a group of coins

What coin has the same value as 5 pennies?

Each penny is worth 1¢.
Count to find the value of 5 pennies.

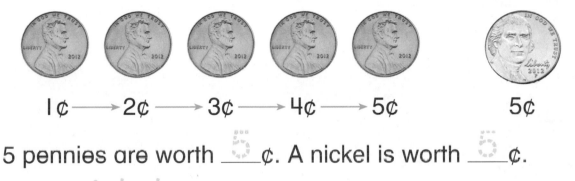

1¢ ⟶ 2¢ ⟶ 3¢ ⟶ 4¢ ⟶ 5¢   5¢

5 pennies are worth __5__¢. A nickel is worth __5__¢.

▷ A __nickel__ has the same value as 5 pennies.

What coin has the same value as 2 nickels?

Each nickel is worth 5¢.

Add to find the
value of 2 nickels.

5¢ + 5¢ = 10¢   10¢

2 nickels are worth __10__¢.

A dime is worth __10__¢.

▷ A __dime__ has the same value as 2 nickels.

Guided Instruction

Connect: What you know about the values of coins

Anna has these two coins.
How many cents are they
worth in all?

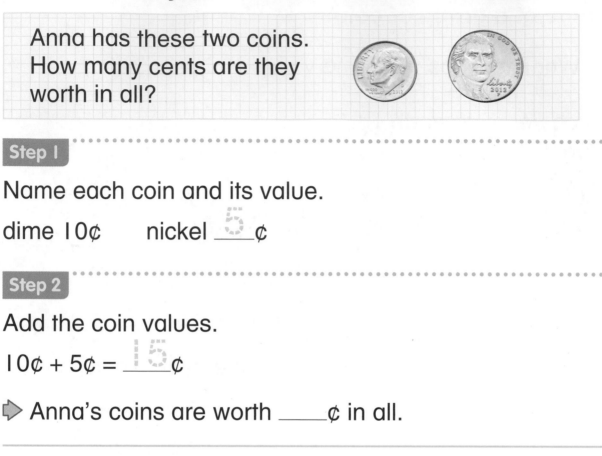

Step 1

Name each coin and its value.

dime 10¢   nickel __5__ ¢

Step 2

Add the coin values.

10¢ + 5¢ = __15__ ¢

➡ Anna's coins are worth ____ ¢ in all.

Ken has two pennies and a nickel.
How much money does Ken have?

Each penny is worth 1¢.
The nickel is worth 5¢.

Add the coin values.

1¢ + 1¢ + 5¢ = __7__ ¢

Ken has ____ ¢ in all.

1. **Rafa wants to buy the scissors.**

   Which group of coins could he use?

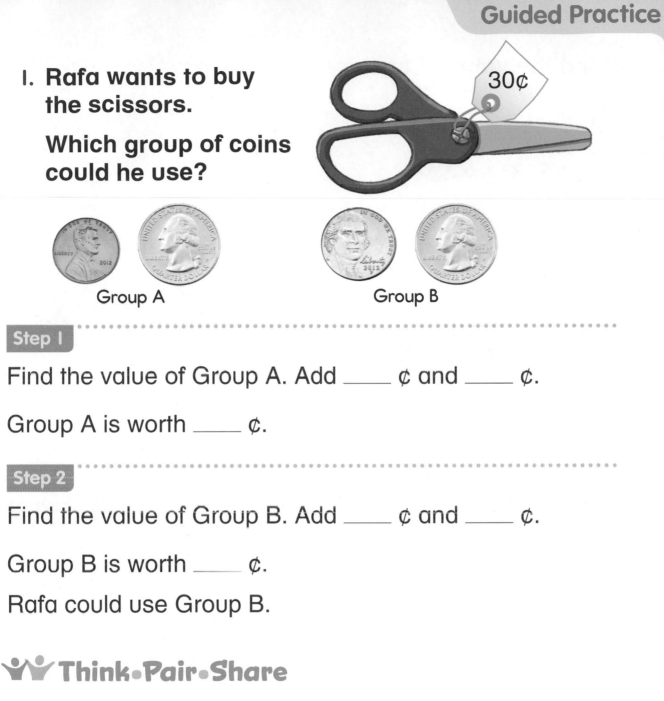

30¢

Group A   Group B

Step 1

Find the value of Group A. Add _____ ¢ and _____ ¢.

Group A is worth _____ ¢.

Step 2

Find the value of Group B. Add _____ ¢ and _____ ¢.

Group B is worth _____ ¢.

Rafa could use Group B.

Think•Pair•Share

MP3 2. Chen has 2 dimes. Can he buy the scissors? Explain your answer.

Independent Practice

Find the value of each group of coins.

1. _____ ¢

2. _____ ¢

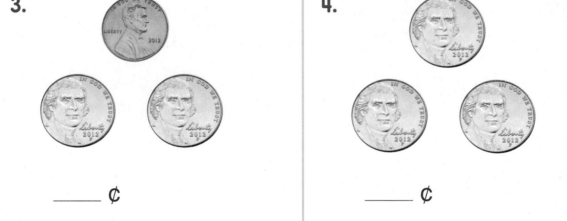

3. _____ ¢

4. _____ ¢

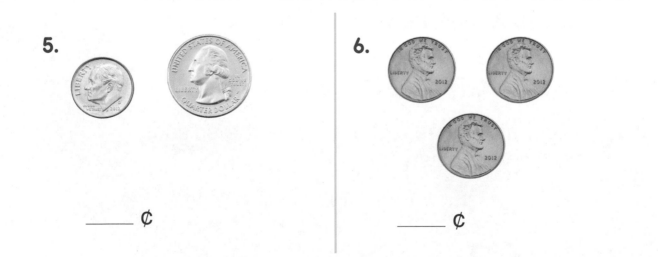

5. _____ ¢

6. _____ ¢

Independent Practice

Circle the group of coins that has the value shown.

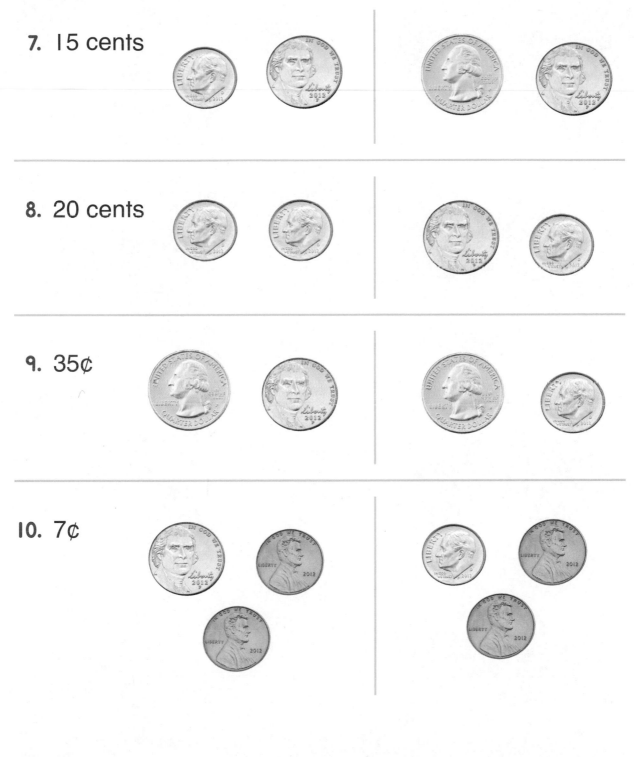

7. 15 cents

8. 20 cents

9. 35¢

10. 7¢

Independent Practice

Write the value of each group of coins.
Match each group of coins to the toy it will buy.

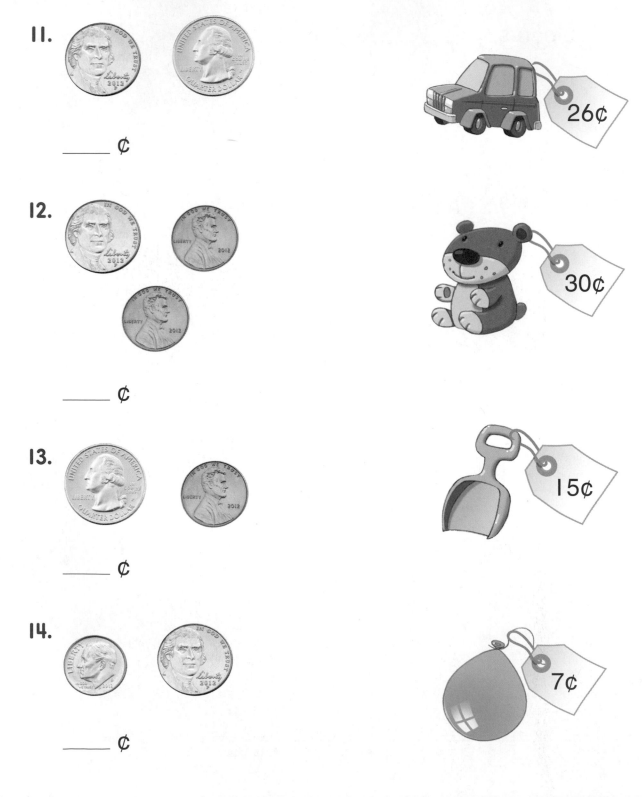

11. _____ ¢

26¢

12. _____ ¢

30¢

13. _____ ¢

15¢

14. _____ ¢

7¢

Independent Practice

MP6 **15.** Elaine has these coins. Count on to find how many cents Elaine has.

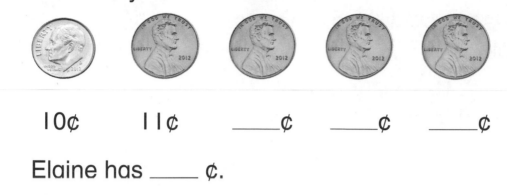

10¢   11¢   ____¢   ____¢   ____¢

Elaine has ____ ¢.

MP6 **16.** Jamal has these coins. Count on to find how many cents Jamal has.

5¢   6¢   ____¢   ____¢   ____¢   ____¢

Jamal has ____ ¢.

MP2 **17.** Tell about three different ways you could make 20¢.

Guided Instruction

Essential Question:
How do you use
a table to make
comparisons?

Words to Know
data
table
tally mark

In this lesson you will learn how to
use a table.

**Understand: Use tally marks to show
data in a table**

The children in Keri's class are using these toys.
Use a table to show how many of each toy the
children are using.

To show data in a table:
Look at the names of the toys in the table.

Look at the pictures. In the
table, make a tally mark for
each picture next to its name.

Draw a line through four
tally marks to make a
bundle of five.

Toy	Number of Toys
Car	卌 II
Train	IIII
Plane	卌 III

⇨ The children are using 7 cars, 4 trains,
and 8 planes.

Understand: **Use a table to find how many in all**

The table shows the number of animals in a pet store.

How many animals are there in all?

Pet	Number of Pets
Cat	ⅢⅠ I
Dog	ⅢⅠ ⅢⅠ
Bird	IIII

Count the tally marks to find how many of each animal.

There are 6 cats, 10 dogs, and 4 birds.

Add to find the total number of animals.

$$6 + 10 + 4 = 20$$

▷ There are 20 animals in all.

Remember!
A line through four tally marks shows a bundle of 5: ⅢⅠ

Understand: **Use a table to compare**

Does the table above show that there are more birds or more cats? How many more?

There are 6 cats and 4 birds. 6 is greater than 4. There are more cats than birds.

Subtract to find how many more. $6 - 4 = 2$

▷ There are 2 more cats than birds.

Guided Instruction

Connect: What you know about showing data in a table

Rosa has these stickers in her album.

Use a table to show how many of each sticker Rosa has.

Step 1

List the kinds of stickers. Look at the pictures.

Make a tally mark for each sticker.

Draw a line through four tally marks to make a bundle of 5.

Sticker	Number of Children
Heart	ⅢⅠ
Happy Face	ⅢⅠ ⅢⅠ Ⅰ
Sun	

Step 2

Count the tally marks for each kind of sticker.

➡ Rosa has _____ heart stickers, _____ happy face

stickers, and _____ sun stickers.

I. **The table shows the favorite sport of some children.**

Sport	Number of Children
Soccer	JHT II
Baseball	JHT JHT I
Basketball	IIII

How many more children chose soccer than chose basketball?

Step I

How many children chose soccer? _____ children

How many children chose basketball? _____ children

Step 2

Subtract to compare. _____ − _____ = _____

_____ more children chose _____.

✶Y✶Think•Pair•Share

MP3 2. Use the table about some children's favorite sport. Write a question that you would use addition to solve.

Tell how you would solve the problem.

Independent Practice

Pat has red, green, and blue beads.

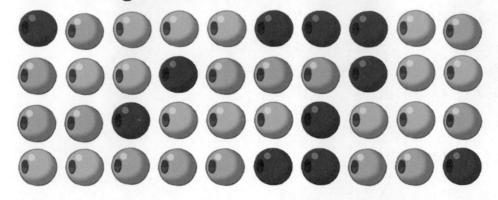

1. Count the beads to complete the table.

Beads	Number of Beads
Red	
Green	
Blue	

2. Are there more red beads or blue beads?

   _____ beads

3. How many green beads are there?

   _____ green beads

4. Which color bead does Pat have the greatest

   number of? _____

Independent Practice

Each child at the school fair was given one balloon. The table shows how many balloons of each color were given out.

Color	Number of Balloons
Red	HHT HHT
Blue	HHT I
Green	III

5. How many children were given blue balloons?

_____ children

6. Which color balloon was given to the most children?

_____

7. How many more children were given blue balloons than were given green balloons?

_____ children

8. How many children were given either a red balloon or a green balloon?

_____ children

Independent Practice

9. **Complete the table to show what some children ate for breakfast.**

Food	Number of Children
Hot cereal	
Cold cereal	
Eggs	

Kyle, Lex, and Sammy ate hot cereal for breakfast. Make tally marks for these children in the table.

Jenny, Maria, Pablo, Nate, and Rob ate cold cereal for breakfast. Make tally marks for these children.

Ana, Luke, Bella, and Zach ate eggs for breakfast. Make tally marks for these children.

Use the table for problems 10–12.

10. Which food did the most children eat for breakfast?

   _____

11. How many more children ate eggs than hot cereal?

   _____

12. How many children ate cereal in all? _____ children

Independent Practice

MP1 **13.** Color some stars blue. Color the rest yellow.

Use your stars. Make tally marks to complete the table.

Color	Number of Stars
Blue	
Yellow	

14. Are there more blue stars or yellow stars?

_____ stars

15. How many more are there?

_____ more

1. Nick and Ella use a ribbon to compare the length across their books. Nick marks the ribbon with a red line to show the length across his Science book. Ella uses the same ribbon to show the length across her Math book.

   Circle the book that has the longer length across. Mark an X on the book that has the shorter length across.

2. Put the objects in order from shortest to longest.

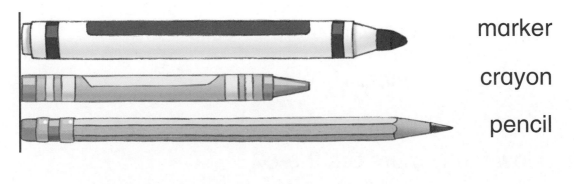

marker

crayon

pencil

_____ , _____ , _____

3. Circle the correct measurement.

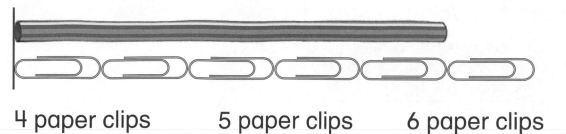

4 paper clips   5 paper clips   6 paper clips

Write the time.

4.

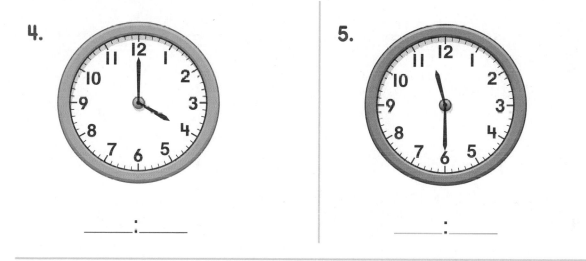

_____:_____

5.

_____:_____

6. Count on to find how many cents in all.

_____ ¢ in all

The table shows the camps that children signed up for this summer.

Camp	Number of Children
Soccer	ⅢⅢ ⅢⅢ ‖
Dance	‖

7. Alex, Ava, Sam, and Julia also signed up for Dance camp. Add tally marks for these children in the table.

8. How many children in all signed up for camp?

_____ children

9. Did more children sign up for Soccer camp or Dance camp? How many more?

_____

MP1 **10.** Kyle draws the hour hand on the clock between the 3 and the 4. Then he draws the minute hand pointing to the 6.

What time does his clock show? Draw hands on the clock to help. Explain how you found the time.

____:____

Progress Check

Look at how the math concepts and skills you have learned and will learn connect.

To practice your skills, go to sadlierconnect.com.

Unit 4

KINDERGARTEN		GRADE 1		GRADE 2
I Can...	Before Unit 4	**Can I ?**	After Unit 4	**I Will...**
Identify shapes in the real world	☐	Understand key attributes of shapes	☐	Recognize and draw shapes with given attributes
Name flat and solid shapes	☐	Build and draw shapes with key attributes	☐	Identify triangles, quadrilaterals, pentagons, hexagons, and cubes
Tell if a shape is flat or solid				
Compare flat shapes				
Compare solid shapes				
Build solid shapes				
Draw flat shapes				
Put together flat shapes to make larger shapes	☐	Put together flat shapes to make new shapes	☐	
	☐	Put together solid shapes to make new shapes	☐	
	☐	Partition shapes into two or four equal shares	☐	Partition a rectangle into same-size squares and count to find total number of squares
	☐	Describe equal shares as halves, fourths, or quarters	☐	Partition shapes into two, three, or four equal shares
	☐	Describe a whole as two or four equal shares	☐	Describe equal shares as halves, thirds, or fourths
				Describe a whole as two halves, three thirds, or four fourths

HOME ◆ CONNECT...

In this unit your child will:

- Identify and compose two-dimensional shapes and three-dimensional shapes.

- Make equal shares.

Ways to Help Your Child

Using literature is a great way to make connections between reading and math. Your local library will contain wonderful resources for books that involve math for first graders. Children's books with math themes are readily available and can enhance what your child is learning in the classroom.

Take advantage of every chance to point out flat and solid shapes in daily life. Encourage your child to notice these shapes both at home and when shopping or doing other chores outside the home. Vacations also provide an excellent opportunity to spot new and unusual flat and solid shapes not normally seen in the family's day-to-day environment.

Your child will identify flat (two-dimensional) and solid (three-dimensional) shapes. They will also make new shapes by combining flat and solid shapes.

Your child will identify a flat shape by its sides and its corners.

- A closed flat shape with 3 straight sides and 3 corners is a triangle.

- A closed flat shape with 4 straight sides and 4 square corners is a rectangle.

- A closed flat shape with 4 straight sides that are the same length and 4 square corners is a square.

Your child will also learn how to partition circles and rectangles into two and four equal parts or shares.

Activity: Play "I Spy a Shape." Challenge your child to find the two-dimensional (flat) or three-dimensional (solid) shapes you describe to them. You might say, "I spy a closed, flat shape with three sides." (Triangle) Since shapes are everywhere, you can play this game whether you are taking a walk, shopping for groceries, or just driving around town.

Focus on Geometry

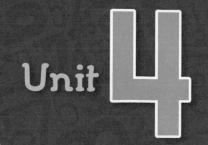

Essential Question:
What shapes do
you see?

Essential Question:
How do you identify triangles and rectangles?

Words to Know
sides
corners
triangle
rectangle
square
trapezoid

Guided Instruction

In this lesson you will learn to identify triangles and rectangles.

Understand: Use sides and corners to identify a triangle

Sophia drew this shape. What is the shape called?

You can identify this shape by its sides and its corners.

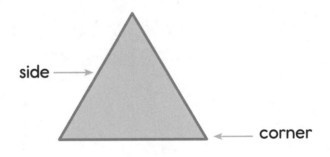

This shape has 3 straight sides and 3 corners.

It is a closed shape. There are no gaps in the sides.

A closed shape with 3 straight sides and 3 corners is a triangle.

⇨ Sophia drew a triangle.

Understand: Use sides and corners to identify a rectangle and a square

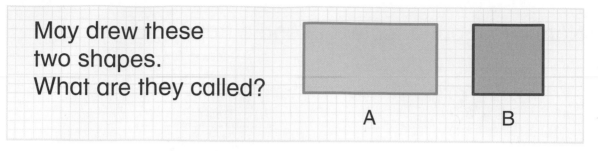

May drew these
two shapes.
What are they called?

A

B

Shape A has 4 straight sides.
It has 4 square corners, like the corners
of this page. It is closed.

A closed shape with 4 straight sides and
4 square corners is a rectangle.

Shape A is a rectangle.

Shape B also has 4 straight sides and
4 square corners. All 4 sides are the same length.
It is closed.

A closed shape with 4 straight sides
that are the same length and 4 square corners
is a square.

Shape B is a square. A square
is a special rectangle.

May drew a rectangle and a _____.

Guided Instruction

Connect: **What you know about identifying shapes**

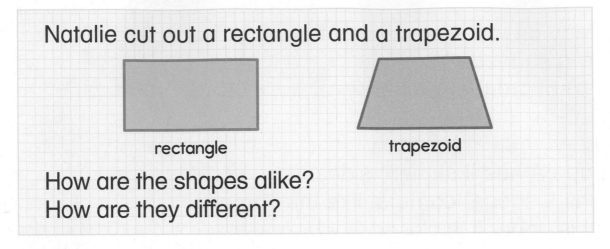

Natalie cut out a rectangle and a trapezoid.

rectangle

trapezoid

How are the shapes alike?
How are they different?

Step 1

Tell how the rectangle and the trapezoid are alike.

Both shapes are ___closed___.

Both shapes have 4 sides and _____ corners.

Step 2

Tell how the shapes are different.
Look at the corners.

The rectangle has 4 ___square___ corners.

The trapezoid does not have square corners.

⇨ Both shapes are closed. Both shapes have
4 sides and 4 corners. The trapezoid does
not have square corners.

Guided Practice

I. Which of these shapes are triangles?

A   B   C

Step 1

Is shape A closed? ____

Does it have 3 straight sides and 3 corners? ____

Is shape A a triangle? ____

Step 2

Does shape B have 3 straight sides? ____

Is shape B a triangle? ____

Step 3

Is shape C closed? ____

Does it have 3 straight sides and 3 corners? ____

Is shape C a triangle? ____

⫷ Think·Pair·Share

MP3 **2.** Shape A and shape C are both triangles.
Talk about how they are different.

Independent Practice

Identify the shapes.
Write *triangle*, *rectangle*, *square*, or *trapezoid*.

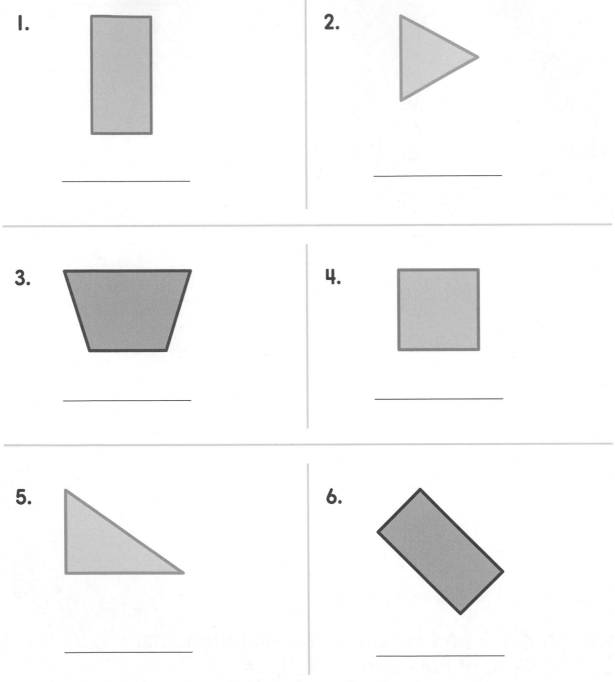

1. _____

2. _____

3. _____

4. _____

5. _____

6. _____

The robot is made of different shapes.
Use the robot for problems 7, 8, and 9.

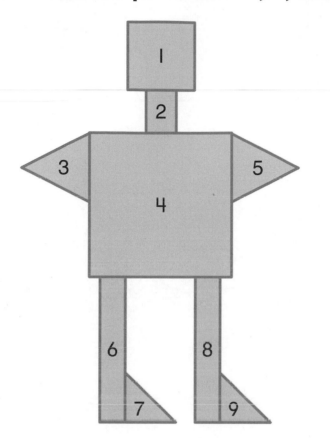

7. Which shapes are triangles? shapes _____

8. Which shapes are rectangles? shapes _____

9. Which shapes are squares? shapes _____

Independent Practice

10. Circle all the rectangles.

11. Circle all the triangles.

12. Circle all the squares.

13. Circle all the trapezoids.

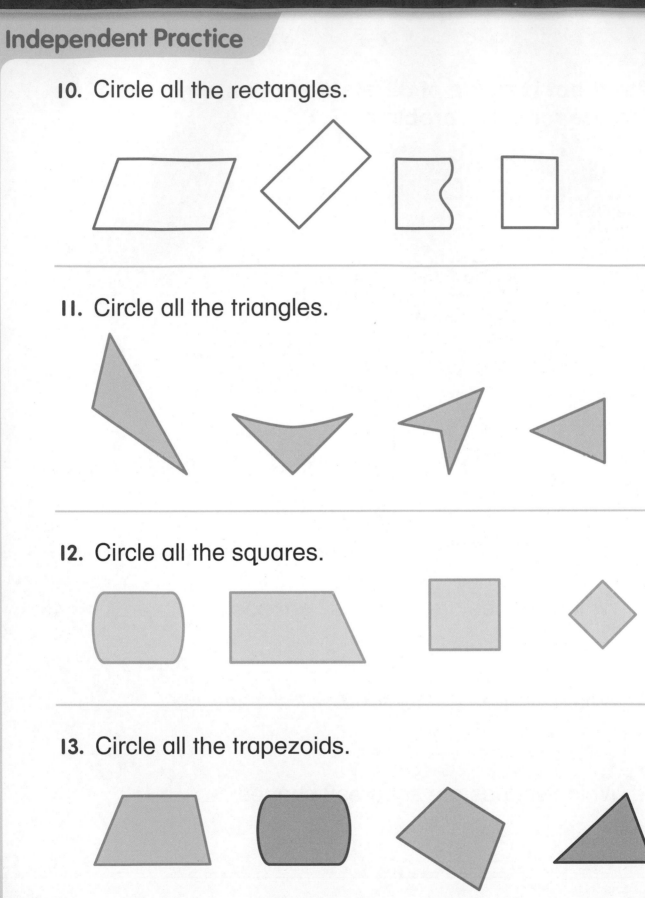

Independent Practice

MP4 **14.** Describe an example of a rectangle and a square in the classroom.

How did you identify the rectangle?

How did you identify the square?

Draw a rectangle and a square.

MP4 **15.** Draw a triangle and a trapezoid.

Jada also drew a triangle and a trapezoid. What must be the same about your shapes and Jada's shapes?

What could be different about your shapes and Jada's shapes?

Essential Question:
How do you put shapes together to make new shapes?

Words to Know
hexagon

Guided Instruction

In this lesson you will learn how to put shapes together to make new shapes.

Understand: Use two squares of the same size to make a rectangle

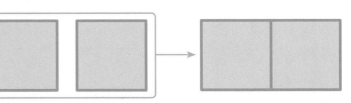

These two squares are the same size, so all the sides match each other.
What shape can you make by joining two sides of these squares?

Put the two squares next to each other.

Join two sides to make a new shape.
The new shape is a rectangle.

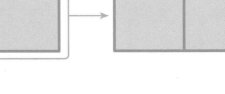

You can also put one square above the other.

Then join two sides to make a new shape. This new shape is also a rectangle.

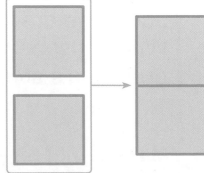

▷ If two squares are the same size, you can join any two sides of the squares to make a rectangle.

Understand: Use two triangles of the same size to make new shapes

These two triangles are the same size. Each has one square corner.
What shapes can you make by joining two matching sides?

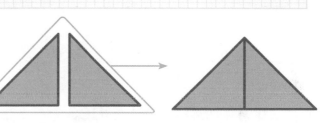

square corner

Join the two triangles along two matching sides as shown.

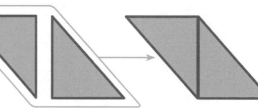

The new shape is a bigger triangle.

Join the triangles along the two longest sides.

The new shape is a rectangle.

Join the two triangles along two matching sides as shown.

The new shape has 4 straight sides and 4 corners that are not square corners.

▷ By joining two matching sides, you can make a bigger triangle, a rectangle, or a new shape with 4 straight sides and 4 corners.

Guided Instruction

Connect: Making shapes with straight sides and making shapes with curved sides

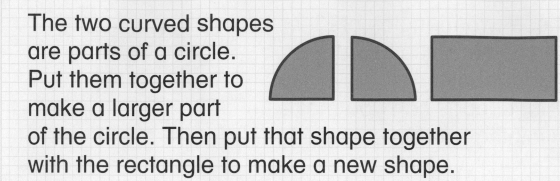

The two curved shapes are parts of a circle. Put them together to make a larger part of the circle. Then put that shape together with the rectangle to make a new shape.

Step 1

Look at the straight sides.
The straight sides match.

Step 2

Put the straight sides together.
The new shape is a larger part
of the circle.

Step 3

Put the new shape from Step 2
together with the rectangle
to make a new shape.

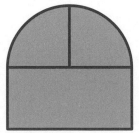
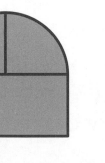

▷ The new shape has a curved
part and some straight sides.

Guided Practice

1. What shapes can you make using the two triangles and the rectangle?

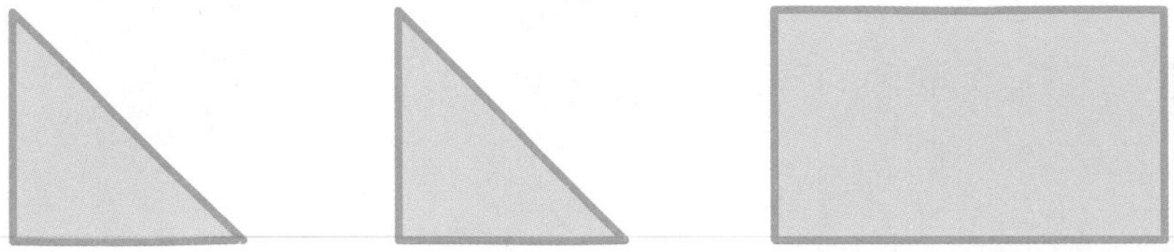

Step 1

Join the triangles to the rectangle along the sides as shown.

Step 2

The new shape has ____ sides.

Is the new shape a square, a rectangle, or a trapezoid?

The new shape is a __________.

Think•Pair•Share

MP1 **2.** You can also make this shape from the triangles and the rectangle.

How is this new shape like the trapezoid above? How is it different from the trapezoid above?

Independent Practice

Draw a circle around the correct new shapes to answer problems 1 and 2.

1. Use these shapes.

Which new shape can you make?

2. Use these shapes.

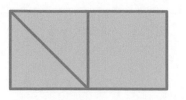

Which new shape can you make?

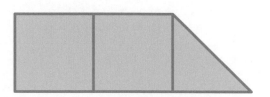

3. This shape is a trapezoid.

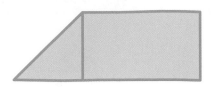

Draw the shapes that were used to make the trapezoid.

4. This shape is a hexagon. It has 6 sides.

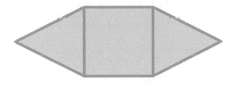

Draw the shapes that were used to make the hexagon.

Independent Practice

5. This shape is also a hexagon.
Circle the shapes that were
used to make this hexagon.

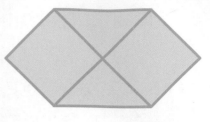

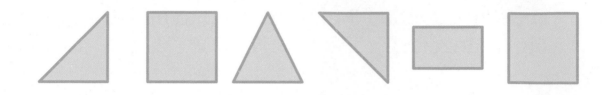

6. Jill has these 3 shapes.

Circle the shapes Jill can make using all 3 shapes.

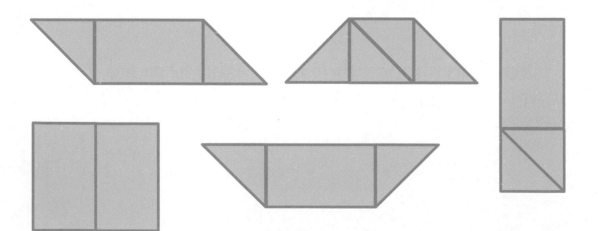

MP5 **7.** This square is made of
4 squares.

Draw a different shape
with the 4 squares.

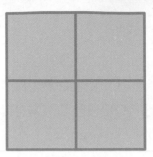

Talk about how you drew the new shape.

MP4 **8.** This square is made of other shapes.

How many triangles are used?____

How many rectangles are used?____

Draw a rectangle with the same shapes.

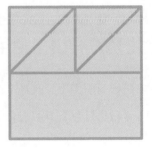

Talk about how you drew the rectangle.

Essential Question:
How do you put solid shapes together to make a new solid shape?

Words to Know
flat shape
cube
solid shape
faces
rectangular prism

Guided Instruction

In this lesson you will learn how to put solid shapes together to make a new solid shape.

Understand: Use two cubes to make a new solid shape

A square is a flat shape. A cube is a solid shape that has 6 square faces.

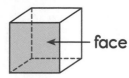

square   cube

What new solid shapes can you make by joining two faces of these cubes?

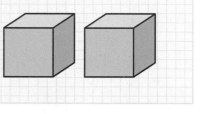

Put the cubes next to each other. Put the faces together.

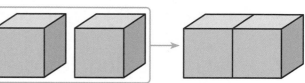

The new solid shape is a rectangular prism. All of its faces are rectangles. Some of the faces are squares.

Remember!
A square is a special kind of rectangle.

Put one cube above the other. The new shape is also a rectangular prism.

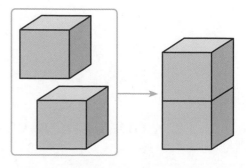

⇨ When two faces of same-size cubes are joined, the new solid shape is a rectangular prism.

Understand: **Use a cube and a rectangular prism to make a new solid shape**

What solid shape can you make by putting together these solid shapes?

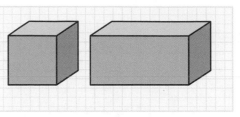

Match two faces that have the same shape.
Put the two faces together.
All the faces of the new solid shape are rectangles.

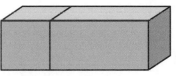

▷ The new solid shape is a rectangular prism.

Understand: **Use curved solid shapes to make a new solid shape**

These solid shapes have three flat faces.
The flat faces are same-size circles. What new solid shape is made by joining two of these faces?

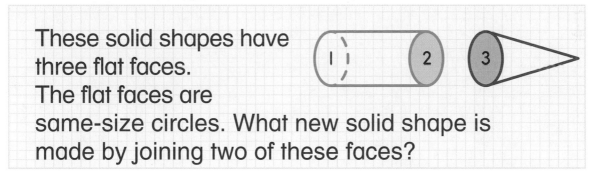

Put the two faces together.

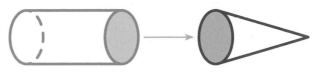

▷ The new solid shape has one flat face that is a circle.

Guided Instruction

Connect: What you know about using solid shapes to make new solid shapes

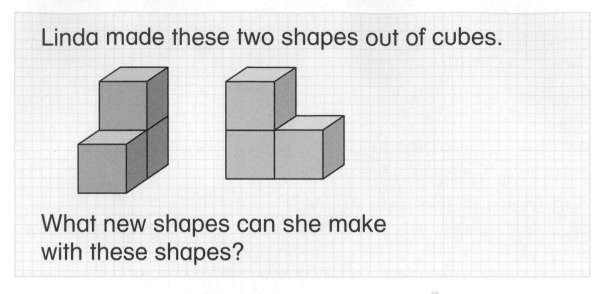

Linda made these two shapes out of cubes.

What new shapes can she make with these shapes?

Make the new shapes by putting the _____ faces _____ together in different ways.

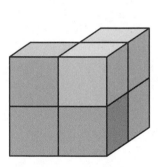
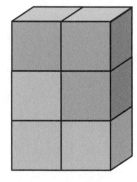
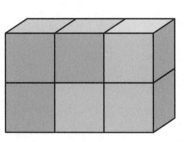

▷ These are some of the shapes Linda can make.

How many cubes are used in each new shape?

_____ cubes

Guided Practice

I. **Orlando built this solid shape with cubes. How many cubes did he use?**

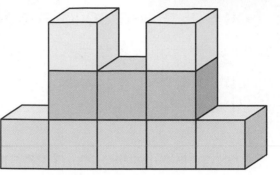

Step 1

Count the cubes in each layer.

How many cubes are in the top layer? ____

How many cubes are in the middle layer? ____

How many cubes are in the bottom layer? ____

Step 2

Add to find the total number of cubes.

____ + ____ + ____ = ____

Orlando used ____ cubes to build the solid shape.

★Think•Pair•Share

2. Orlando also made this shape. Talk about how this shape is like the other shape. Talk about how it is different.

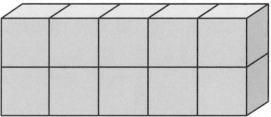

Independent Practice

1. Look at these solid shapes.

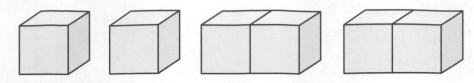

Circle the new solid shape below that can be made by using all the solid shapes above.

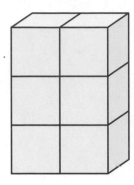   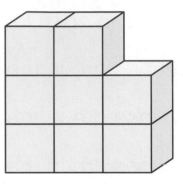

---

2. Look at these cubes.

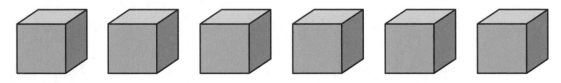

Circle the new solid shape below that can be made by using all the cubes above.

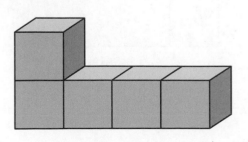

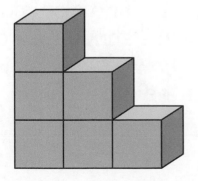

3. Look at these solid shapes.

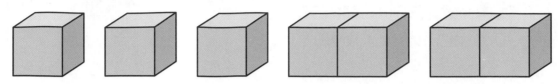

Circle the new solid shape below that can be made by using all the solid shapes above.

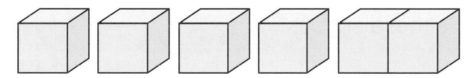

4. Look at these solid shapes.

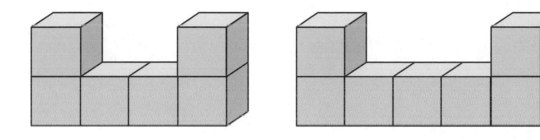

Circle the new solid shape below that can be made by using all the solid shapes above.

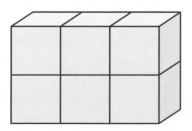 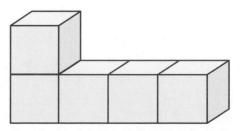

Independent Practice

5. Pam and Jay used
different solid shapes
to build this shape.

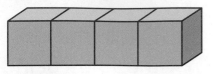

Pam used this shape.

How many did she use? _____

Jay used this shape.

How many did he use? _____

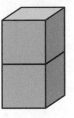

6. Jacob wants to make
this shape.

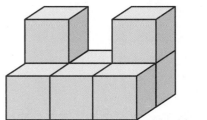

He has these shapes.

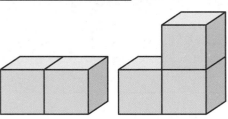

What other shape does he need?
Circle the answer.

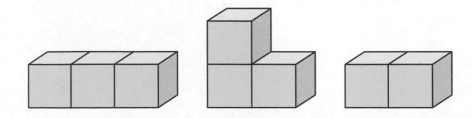

MP7 **7.** Look at these solid shapes.

Solid A   Solid B

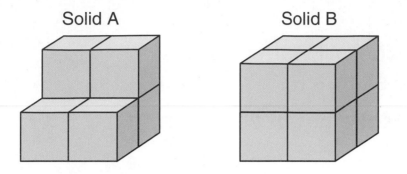

Talk about how these solid shapes are alike and how they are different.

MP2 **8.** This solid shape is made from 4 cubes.

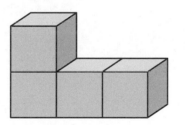

Talk about how you could move the cubes to make two other solid shapes.

Partition Shapes into Equal Shares

Essential Question:
How do you make equal shares?

Words to Know
equal share
halves
half
fourth
quarter

Guided Instruction

In this lesson you will learn how to make equal shares.

Understand: Make equal shares of a circle

This circle has the same shape as a whole pizza.

How can 2 friends share the pizza equally?

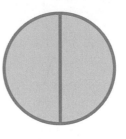

Cut the whole circle into 2 equal parts. Each equal part is an equal share of the circle.

The circle is cut into halves. Each equal share is one half of the circle. There are 2 halves in the whole circle.

▷ Two friends can share the pizza equally when it is cut into 2 halves.

Guided Instruction

Understand: **Make equal shares of a square**

Ms. Carter has a square sheet of paper. How can she share the paper equally among 4 children?

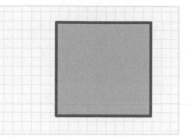

Here is one way to share the paper equally among 4 children.

The whole square has 4 equal parts. Each equal part is one fourth of the whole.

A fourth is also called a quarter. There are 4 quarters in a whole.

Here is another way to share the paper equally among 4 children.

The whole square has 4 equal parts. Each equal part is one fourth, or one quarter, of the whole. There are 4 fourths, or 4 quarters, in the whole.

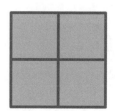

▷ Ms. Carter can use either way to share the paper equally among 4 children. Each child will get 1 fourth of the whole sheet of paper.

Guided Instruction

Connect: **What you know about equal shares**

The two rectangles are cut into equal shares.

Rectangle A   Rectangle B

How many halves are in rectangle A?
How many fourths are in rectangle B?

Step 1

How many equal shares is rectangle A cut into? _2_

Each share is ___1 half___ of the whole.

Color 1 half of rectangle A.

➡ There are ___ halves in rectangle A.

Step 2

How many equal shares is rectangle B cut into? ___

Each share is ___1 fourth___ of the whole.

Color 1 fourth of rectangle B.

➡ There are ___ fourths in rectangle B.

I. Angelina cuts 3 pancakes into pieces.

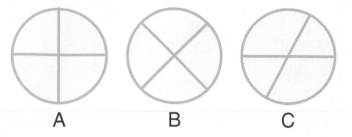

A   B   C

Which pancakes are cut into quarters?

Step I

Which pancakes are cut into 4 equal shares?

_____

Step 2

Is one share of pancake A a quarter of the whole? _____

Is one share of pancake B a quarter of the whole?

Step 3

Which pancakes are cut into quarters? _____

☆ Think•Pair•Share

MP4

2. Draw a pizza and cut it into 4 unequal shares.

Is each share a quarter of the pizza? Explain your answer.

Independent Practice

1. Use the rectangle.

There are _____ equal shares.

Each equal share is a _____ of the whole rectangle.

There are _____ halves.

Color half of the rectangle.

2. Use the circle.

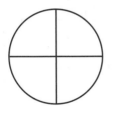

There are _____ equal shares.

Each equal share is a _____ of the whole circle.

There are _____ fourths.

There are _____ quarters.

Color a quarter of the circle.

Independent Practice

Draw lines to cut each shape into halves.

3.

4.

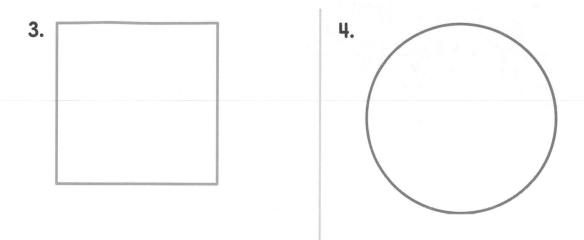

Draw lines to cut each shape into quarters.

5.

6.

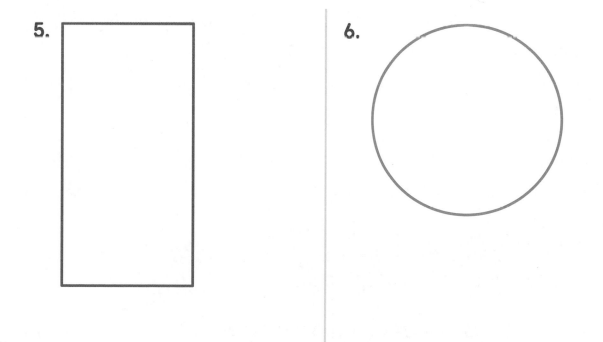

Independent Practice

Use the rectangles for problems 7 – 10.

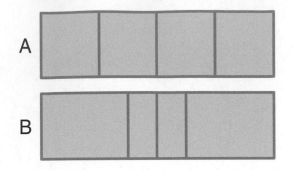

7. Is rectangle A cut into equal shares? _____

8. Is rectangle B cut into equal shares? _____

9. How many quarters are in rectangle A? _____

10. Each share of rectangle A is a _____
of the whole.

11. These rectangles are the same size. Which is larger,
a fourth of the rectangle or a half of the rectangle?

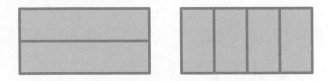

A _____ of the rectangle is larger than a _____
of the rectangle.

Independent Practice

MP1 **12.** You can cut other shapes into equal shares.
Draw lines to cut each shape into halves.

Talk about how you know each shape is
cut into 2 halves.

MP6 **13.** Show 2 different ways to cut these rectangles
into quarters.

Talk about how you know each rectangle is
cut into quarters.

1. Circle all the trapezoids.

2. Circle all the rectangles.

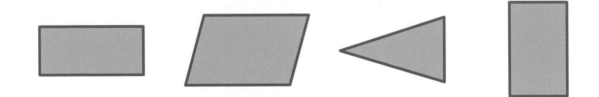

Devon and Ryan used different solid shapes to build this shape.

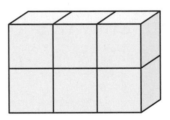

3. Devon used this shape.

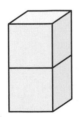

How many of these shapes did he use? _____

4. Ryan used this shape.

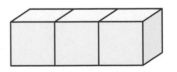

How many of these shapes did he use? _____

Use the circle for problems 5–7.

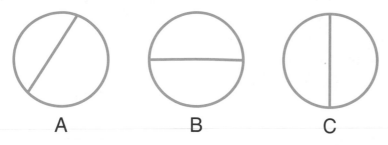

A   B   C

5. Is Circle A cut into equal shares? _____

6. How many halves are in Circle B? _____

7. Color a half of Circle C.

8. Circle the shapes used to make this hexagon.

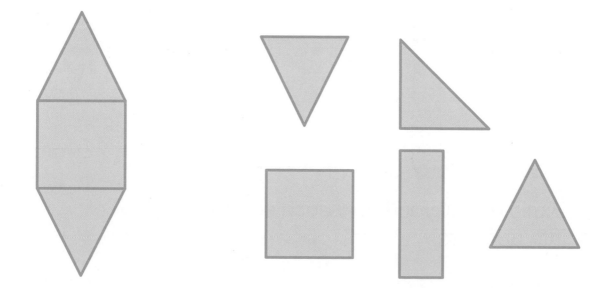

MP7 **9.** Draw a triangle.

Mia also drew a triangle.
What <u>must</u> be true about your triangle and
Mia's triangle?

What could be different about your triangle
and Mia's triangle?

MP6 **10.** Show two different ways to cut these squares
into quarters.

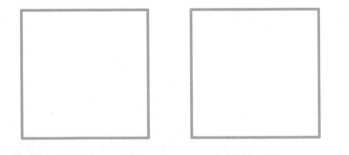

Explain how you know each square is cut
into quarters.

Performance Tasks

Performance Tasks show your understanding of the math that you have learned.

Beginning This Task

This is the beginning of a Performance Task. The next three pages have problems for you to solve.

As you work, you will:

1. Show that you can use math skills and concepts.

2. Decide how to solve a problem.

3. Use different ways to model and solve real-world problems.

Tips to help you!

- Read each problem carefully.
- Plan how you will solve the problem.
- Check your work.
- Be ready to show your work or explain your thinking.

Art Class

I. Art class is today. Everybody will make a drawing. How about drawing some worms?

a. Draw a blue worm, a red worm, and a green worm. Make each one a different length.

blue worm

red worm

green worm

b. Order your worms from shortest to longest.

_____ worm, _____ worm, _____ worm

2. Tina cuts out these clay shapes.

She makes a table to show the shapes and how many of each shape she cut out.

a. Complete the table.

Shape	Number Cut Out
△	ⵑⵑⵑⵑ |||
◯	
▢	

b. How many shapes did Tina cut out in all? Write an equation to find how many shapes she cut out in all.

____ + ____ + ____ = ____

Tina cut out ____ shapes in all.

3. Dan is making a wooden puzzle. He wants to cut the puzzle into fourths. Draw three different models of a puzzle Dan could make.

a. Make one model a circle.

b. Make one model a square.

c. Make one model a rectangle.

d. If Dan had cut his puzzle into halves, would the equal shares be larger or smaller than the fourths he made? Talk about how you know.

_____

Foundational Skills Handbook

Number Names and Counting

	❋	❋ ❋	❋ ❋ ❋	❋ ❋ ❋ ❋	❋ ❋ ❋ ❋ ❋
0	1	2	3	4	5
zero	one	two	three	four	five

❋ ❋ ❋ ❋ ❋ ❋	❋ ❋ ❋ ❋ ❋ ❋ ❋	❋ ❋ ❋ ❋ ❋ ❋ ❋ ❋	❋ ❋ ❋ ❋ ❋ ❋ ❋ ❋ ❋	❋ ❋ ❋ ❋ ❋ ❋ ❋ ❋ ❋ ❋
6	7	8	9	10
six	seven	eight	nine	ten

Match.

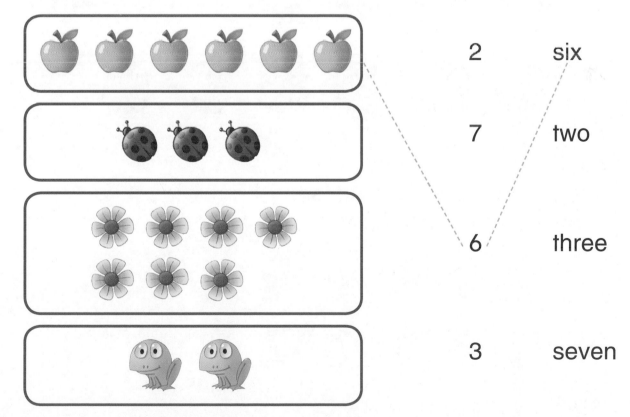

Comparing Numbers

5

3

5 is greater than 3.
3 is less than 5.

Draw lines to compare.
Circle the number that is greater.

1.

4

6

Draw lines to compare.
Circle the number that is less.

2.

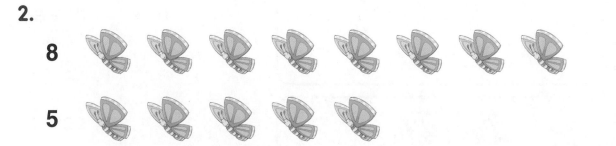

8

5

Addition

There are 2 fish.
Then 1 more fish comes.
How many fish are there now?

$$2 + 1 = 3$$

There are 3 fish now.

Add.

1. There are 3 red balloons and 1 blue balloon.
How many balloons are there in all?

$$3 + 1 = \rule{1cm}{0.15mm}$$

There are _____ balloons in all.

2. There are 4 birds in the yard.
Then 3 more birds come.
How many birds are there now?

$$4 + 3 = \rule{1cm}{0.15mm}$$

There are _____ birds now.

Subtraction

There are 4 birds. Then 1 flies away.
How many birds are there now?

$$4 - 1 = 3$$

There are 3 birds now.

Subtract.

1. There are 4 butterflies. Then 2 fly away.
   How many butterflies are there now?

$$4 - 2 = \underline{\quad}$$

There are _____ butterflies now.

2. There are 7 flowers in the garden.
   Raj picks 4 flowers. How many flowers are left?

$$7 - 4 = \underline{\quad}$$

There are _____ flowers left.

Make Names for Numbers

Make names for 3.
Use red and yellow counters.

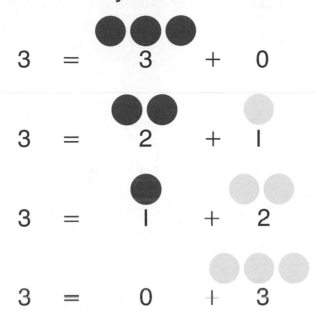

3 = 3 + 0

3 = 2 + 1

3 = 1 + 2

3 = 0 + 3

Color the counters and write the numbers.

1. Make two names for 5.

5 = ____ + ____   5 = ____ + ____

2. Make two names for 9.

○ ○ ○ ○ ○
○ ○ ○ ○

○ ○ ○ ○
○ ○ ○ ○ ○

9 = ____ + ____   9 = ____ + ____

Make a Ten

8 and how many more make 10?

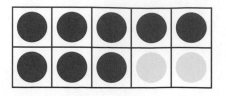

8 and 2 more make 10.

$8 + 2 = 10$

Make a ten.

1.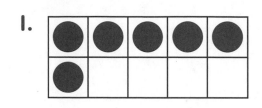

6 and ____ more make 10.

$6 +$ ____ $= 10$

2.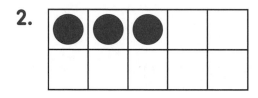

3 and ____ more make 10.

$3 +$ ____ $= 10$

3.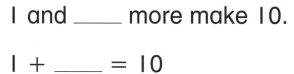

1 and ____ more make 10.

$1 +$ ____ $= 10$

4.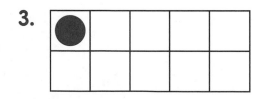

5 and ____ more make 10.

$5 +$ ____ $= 10$

Facts to 5

$$1 + 1 = 2$$

$$3 - 1 = 2$$

Add or subtract.

1. $3 + 1 = $ _____

2. $3 + 2 = $ _____

3. $4 - 1 = $ _____

4. $5 - 0 = $ _____

5. $1 + 2 = $ _____

6. $3 - 3 = $ _____

7. $5 - 3 = $ _____

8. $1 + 4 = $ _____

9.
$$\begin{array}{r} 2 \\ +2 \\ \hline \end{array}$$

10.
$$\begin{array}{r} 2 \\ -1 \\ \hline \end{array}$$

11.
$$\begin{array}{r} 2 \\ +3 \\ \hline \end{array}$$

12.
$$\begin{array}{r} 4 \\ -3 \\ \hline \end{array}$$

Numbers 11–19

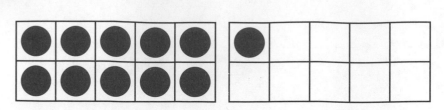

$$10 + 1 = 11$$

10 and 1 more make 11.

How many do you add to 10 to make each number?

1. Make 14.

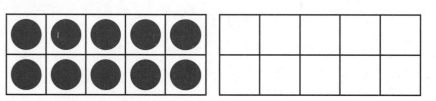

10 and _____ more make 14.

10 + _____ = 14

2. Make 19.

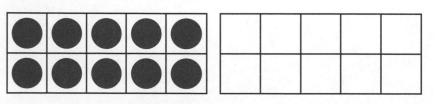

10 and _____ more make 19.

10 + _____ = 19

Measurement

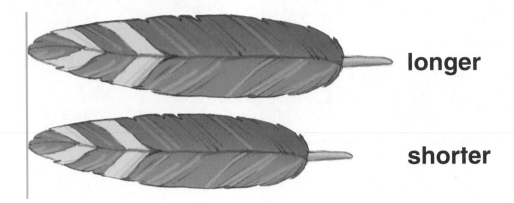

longer

shorter

Which is longer? Draw a circle around it.

1.

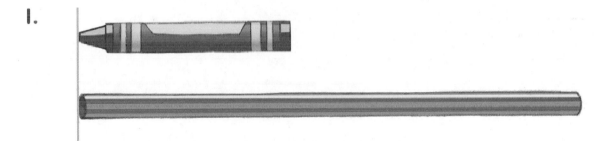

Which is shorter? Draw a circle around it.

2.

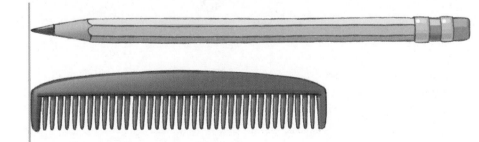

Geometry and Data

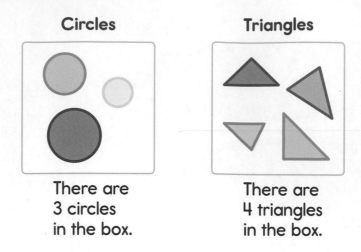

Circles

There are
3 circles
in the box.

Triangles

There are
4 triangles
in the box.

1. Match each shape to the correct box.

3 sides

4 sides

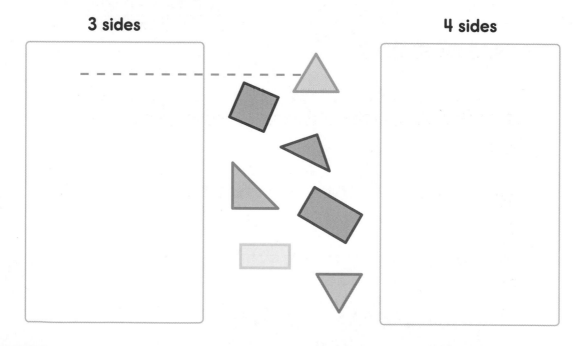

2. How many shapes with 3 sides are there? _____

3. How many shapes with 4 sides are there? _____

You can use this model to solve problems.

Read

Read the problem.
- What facts do you know?
- What do you need to find?

Plan

Plan how to solve the problem.
- Will you add or subtract?
- Will you draw a picture?
- Is the problem a one-step or two-step problem?

Solve

Use your plan to solve the problem.
- Did you answer the question?
- Did you label your answer?

Check

Make sure your answer makes sense.
- How can you solve the problem a different way?
- Is the answer the same?

A Shell Problem

Tina has some shells.
Her friend gives her 9 more shells.
Then Tina has 17 shells in all.
How many shells did Tina have at the start?

Read

What facts do you know?
Tina's friend gives her 9 shells.
Tina has 17 shells in all.

What do you need to find?
How many shells Tina had at the start

Plan

Make a drawing. The number in all is 17.
One addend is 9. Find the missing addend.

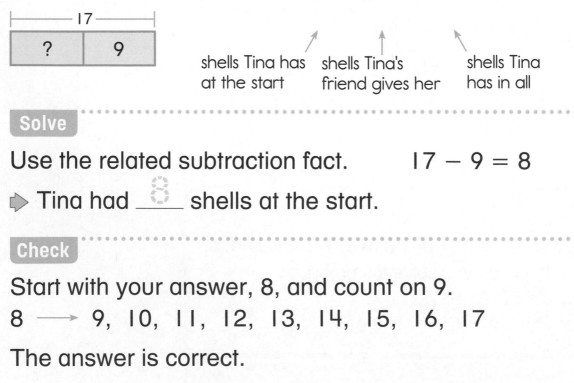

17	
?	9

shells Tina has at the start

shells Tina's friend gives her

shells Tina has in all

Solve

Use the related subtraction fact. $17 - 9 = 8$

➡ Tina had __8__ shells at the start.

Check

Start with your answer, 8, and count on 9.
8 ⟶ 9, 10, 11, 12, 13, 14, 15, 16, 17

The answer is correct.

A Saving Quarters Problem

Lily saved 15 quarters.
Jay saved 4 fewer quarters than Lily.
How many quarters did Jay save?

What facts do you know?
Lily saved 15 quarters.
Jay saved 4 fewer than Lily.

What do you need to find?
How many quarters Jay saved

Plan

The word *fewer* means not as many.
Write a subtraction sentence.

$$15 - 4 = \blacksquare$$

number of   difference between   number of
quarters   Lily's number and   quarters
Lily saved   Jay's number   Jay saved

Solve

$15 - 4 = 11$ ____ is 4 fewer than 15.

➡ Jay saved ____ quarters.

Check

Use the related addition sentence. $11 + 4 = 15$
The answer is correct.

Standards for Mathematical Practice

The Standards for Mathematical Practice, identified here, are an important part of learning mathematics. They are covered in every lesson in this book.

MP1 **Make sense of problems and persevere in solving them.**

- Analyze and plan a solution
- Relate to a similar problem
- Assess progress
- Use concrete objects or pictures
- Check solutions

MP2 **Reason abstractly and quantitatively.**

- Pay attention to all mathematical language
- Represent problems using symbols
- Consider units in problem solving
- Use properties of operations and objects

MP3 **Construct viable arguments and critique the reasoning of others.**

- Analyze a problem situation
- Share reasoning with others
- Explain an approach to a problem
- Construct arguments by using drawings or concrete objects

MP4 **Model with mathematics.**

- Relate mathematics to everyday problems
- Make assumptions and estimations
- Explain the relationship of quantities
- Use concrete tools to explain operations
- Interpret the solution in the context of a situation

MP5 **Use appropriate tools strategically.**

- Consider the range of available tools (e.g., place-value charts, graphs, clocks, etc.)
- Decide on appropriate tools to use for each situation
- Use tools carefully and strategically

MP6 **Attend to precision.**

- Communicate with precision
- Identify the meaning of symbols
- Use measurement units appropriately
- Calculate accurately
- Carefully formulate full explanations

MP7 **Look for and make use of structure.**

- Search for patterns or structure
- Evaluate the structure or design of a problem
- Discuss geometric shapes in terms of their similarities and differences

MP8 **Look for and express regularity in repeated reasoning.**

- Make generalizations in computation
- Obtain fluency using patterns
- Look for patterns with shapes and designs
- Use patterns to relate operations
- Evaluate reasonableness of answers

Key: MP = Mathematical Practice

260 **Standards for Mathematical Practice**

A

add to find how many in all

2   +   3   = 5

---

addends the numbers you add

$$4 + 1 = 5$$
addends

$$\begin{array}{r} 3 \\ +7 \\ \hline 10 \end{array}$$ addends

C

cent a unit used for money

3 cents   5 cents

---

clock

column

column ↓

1	2	3	4	5	6	7	8	9	10
11	12	13	14	15	16	17	18	19	20
21	22	23	24	25	26	27	28	29	30
31	32	33	34	35	36	37	38	39	40
41	42	43	44	45	46	47	48	49	50
51	52	53	54	55	56	57	58	59	60
61	62	63	64	65	66	67	68	69	70
71	72	73	74	75	76	77	78	79	80
81	82	83	84	85	86	87	88	89	90
91	92	93	94	95	96	97	98	99	100

corner

← corner

corner →

count on   start at one number and count in order

4 ⟶ 5 6 7

4 + 3 = 7

cube

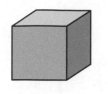

D

digits 1, 2, 3, 4, 5, 6, 7, 8, 9, 0 are used to write numbers

2 4
↑ ↑
digits

dime a coin worth 10 cents, or 10¢

10 cents

doubles

3 + 3 = 6

doubles plus 1

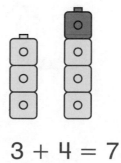

3 + 4 = 7

equal share

Each rectangle shows 4 equal shares.

equal sign (=) is equal to

$$1 + 1 = 2$$

↑
is equal to

equation a number sentence with an equal sign

$$5 + 6 = 11 \qquad 8 - 6 = 2$$

F

face a flat side of a solid shape

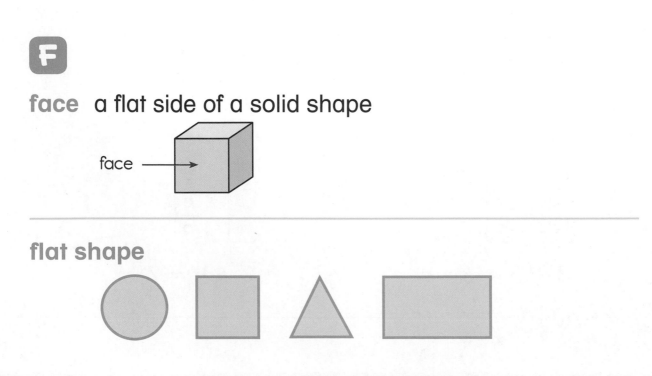

face ⟶

flat shape

fourth   The rectangle is in fourths.

I fourth, or I quarter, is shaded.

greater than (>)   is greater than

13 is greater than 12

13   >   12

half   The rectangle is cut in half.

I half is shaded.

half hour   There are 30 minutes in a half hour.

halves   2 halves make a whole

2 halves are shaded. I whole circle is shaded.

hexagon   a flat shape with 6 sides and 6 corners

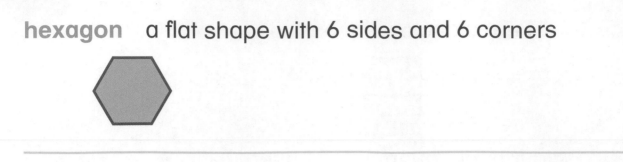

---

hour   There are 60 minutes in 1 hour.

---

hour hand   the shorter hand on a clock, shows the hour

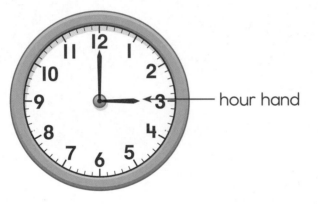

hour hand

length   how long an object is

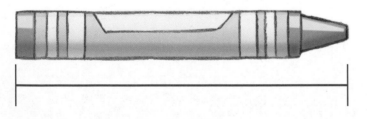

---

less than (<)   is less than

13 is less than 22

13 < 22

minute There are 60 minutes in I hour.

---

minute hand the longer hand on a clock, shows the minutes

minute hand

nickel a coin worth 5 cents, or 5¢

5 cents

---

number names the word name for a number

26
twenty-six ⟵ number name

ones

35 has 5 ones.

penny   a coin worth 1 cent, or 1¢

1 cent

place-value chart   a chart that shows the value of each digit

tens	ones
6	4

64 is 6 tens and 4 ones.

quarter   a coin worth 25 cents, or 25¢

25 cents

rectangle   a flat shape with 4 sides and 4 corners

rectangular prism

related facts   facts that have the same numbers

7 + 6 = 13   13 − 6 = 7

6 + 7 = 13   13 − 7 = 6

These four facts are related facts.

row

1	2	3	4	5	6	7	8	9	10
11	12	13	14	15	16	17	18	19	20
21	22	23	24	25	26	27	28	29	30
31	32	33	34	35	36	37	38	39	40
41	42	43	44	45	46	47	48	49	50
51	52	53	54	55	56	57	58	59	60
61	62	63	64	65	66	67	68	69	70
71	72	73	74	75	76	77	78	79	80
81	82	83	84	85	86	87	88	89	90
91	92	93	94	95	96	97	98	99	100

row →

side

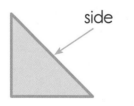

side

solid shape

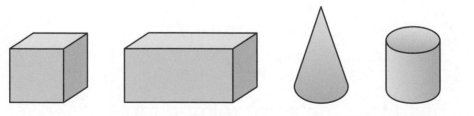

square a flat shape with 4 equal sides and 4 corners

subtract to find how many are left

$$5 - 2 = 3$$

sum the answer in addition

$$4 + 3 = 7 \longleftarrow \text{sum}$$

table

Favorite Sport	Number of Children
Soccer	~~IIII~~ ~~IIII~~ II
Basketball	III
Baseball	~~IIII~~ III

tally mark marks used to show how many

I means I   ~~IIII~~ means 5

tens

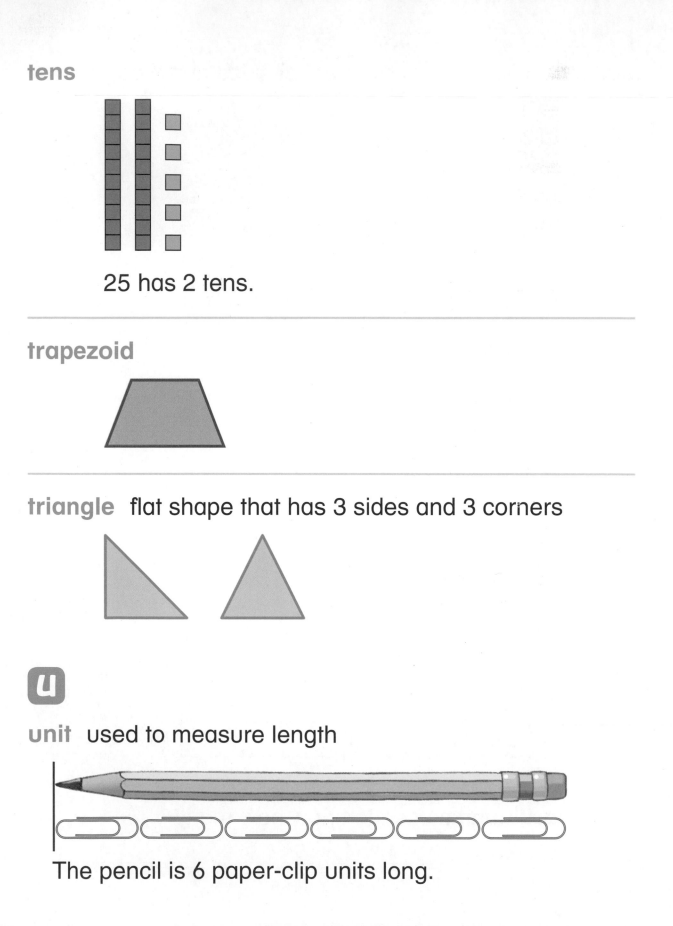

25 has 2 tens.

trapezoid

triangle flat shape that has 3 sides and 3 corners

u

unit used to measure length

The pencil is 6 paper-clip units long.